Indicting Israel

New York Times coverage
of the Palestinian-Israeli conflict

A July 1–December 31, 2011 Study

CAMERA Monograph Series

A Publication of CAMERA,
Committee for Accuracy in Middle East Reporting in America
Boston, Massachusetts

CAMERA, the Committee for Accuracy in Middle East Reporting in America, is a national media-monitoring organization founded in 1982 that works to promote more accurate, balanced and complete coverage of Israel and the Middle East. Aware of the vital role of the mass media in shaping public perception and public policy, CAMERA seeks to educate both journalists and news consumers about the complex issues related to achievement of peace in the Middle East. CAMERA is a non-profit, tax-exempt organization under section 501(c)(3) of the United States Internal Revenue Code.

Published by The Committee for Accuracy in Middle East Reporting in America
CAMERA
P.O. Box 35040
Boston, MA 02135

ISBN 978-0-9661548-7-0

CONTENTS

Executive Summary

Background

The New York Times remains one of the most influential newspapers in the world. Its print and Web versions are read and relied upon by millions, including highly-educated news consumers and opinion-shapers in America and around the globe. Dubbed the "newspaper of record," *The Times* sets the topic and the tone for many other print and electronic media outlets. Its editorial decisions—what it deems most newsworthy, what it chooses to ignore or consign to back pages and how it frames the stories it covers—substantially shape the news landscape and, in turn, public perception of events. Given this, its presentation of the complex Palestinian-Israeli conflict is obviously of great importance and any pattern of bias must be taken seriously.

CAMERA's investigation of *New York Times* coverage between July 1 and Dec. 31, 2011 reveals empirically that there is real cause for concern. The dominant finding of the study is a disproportionate, continuous, embedded indictment of Israel that dominates both news and commentary sections. Israeli views are downplayed while Palestinian perspectives, especially criticism of Israel, are amplified and even promoted. The net effect is an overarching message, woven into the fabric of the coverage, of Israeli fault and responsibility for the conflict.

When *The Times* presents criticism of Israel more than twice as often as it does criticism of the Palestinians, when it features the Palestinian perspective on the peace process nearly twice as often as it does the Israeli perspective, when it consistently omits the context of Israel's blockade of Gaza, when it rehashes the actions of the Israeli military aboard a Turkish ship but leaves out the precipitating violence by pro-Palestinian activists, and when it de-emphasizes Palestinian aggression and incitement while headlining Israeli defensive strikes, readers can be profoundly deceived about the realities. And when other media outlets emulate *The Times*, the effect of the distortion is greatly magnified.

Such negative and skewed treatment of the Jewish state is not new. It follows a long history of *The New York Times* distorting the news to avoid the appearance of espousing so-called Jewish causes. In her book *Buried by* The Times: *The Holocaust and America's Most Important Newspaper,* Northeastern University journalism professor Laurel Leff described how *The New York Times* deliberately downplayed news about Nazi persecution and the genocide of European Jews. According to Leff, the decision to avoid presenting Jews as victims of Hitler was consciously made by the publisher to ensure the newspaper would not appear "too Jewish."[1] Former *Times* Executive Editor Max Frankel said the same in a 2001 article, in which he lamented the "staggering, staining failure of *The New York Times* to depict Hitler's methodical extermination of the Jews of Europe as a horror beyond all other horrors in World War II ...." He noted that publisher Arthur Hayes Sulzberger "went to great lengths to avoid having *The Times* branded a 'Jewish newspaper.'"[2]

The same mind-set continued to shape the news years later. Columbia University journalism professor Ari L. Goldman, a former *New York Times* reporter, recounted how his dispatches about the 1991 violence by African-Americans against Jews in

Crown Heights were altered to fit the "frame" preferred by editors, who transformed them into stories about a purported race war between blacks and whites instead of the anti-Jewish attacks that Goldman had witnessed and described.[3]

A similar pattern of minimizing threats to Jews was documented in CAMERA's 2002 study, "*The New York Times* Skews Israeli-Palestinian Crisis," which exposed the newspaper's distorted emphasis on alleged wrongdoing by the Jewish state during a period of unprecedented terrorism against Israel. While amplifying news of Israeli military responses, it ignored or minimized Palestinian attacks.[4] The message was clear—Israel was culpable.

Ten years later, the message is the same.

The Study

The study examines all news and editorial content in the print edition of the newspaper directly relating to the Palestinian-Israeli conflict. As has been its habit over many years, *The New York Times* made the Palestinian-Israeli conflict a central focus of its foreign coverage during the six months studied.[5] This was not a period of extraordinary crisis and turmoil in Israel, yet nearly 200 news stories dealt with Palestinian-Israeli strife. There were 20 opinion pieces over a period of nine months regarding the conflict.

Criticism of Israel is found to be a pervasive motif, continuously woven into the reportage. The Jewish state is criticized more than twice as often as the Palestinians. Of 275 passages in the news pages classified as criticism according to the study's stringent criteria (detailed in Appendix I), 187 were critical of Israel; fewer than half as many—88—were critical of the Palestinians. Some of these criticisms were expressed in the voices of the journalists themselves, often in violation of professional norms against editorializing in news reporting. Journalists weighed in 21 times with hostile views of Israel, and only 9 times with criticism of the Palestinians.

But the broader numerical discrepancy in criticism does not by itself tell the entire story. The study, therefore, zooms in on specific topics within the newspaper's coverage of the Palestinian-Israeli conflict to reveal a consistent double standard in the *Times'* rendering of events.

Among the topics frequently discussed on the news pages and analyzed in the study during the second half of 2011 were:

The Peace Process and Palestinian Unilateral Declaration of Independence (UDI)

Palestinian points of view about peace talks and the Palestinian Authority's unilateral campaign for recognition at the United Nations significantly overshadowed Israeli points of view, with 106 passages presenting a mainstream Palestinian perspective on the topic but only 59 passages presenting a mainstream Israeli viewpoint. Although both sides obviously held strong opinions on the peace process, as well as on the merits or demerits of the Palestinian resort to unilateralism, the newspaper did not present each side's views as equally newsworthy and chose instead to highlight Palestinian opinion.

The Mavi Marmara

The newspaper's reporting about the *Mavi Marmara*, a Turkish ship carrying pro-Palestinian activists, lacked crucial context and relayed criticism in a lopsided manner. Of 37 articles that referenced Israel's use of force on the ship, only 8 mentioned the activists' violence that necessitated the use of firearms by Israeli commandos. Twenty passages conveyed criticism of Israel's actions relating to the *Mavi Marmara* incident, and only 5 conveyed criticism of the pro-Palestinian activists on board. Even when describing a U.N. report that criticized both sides in roughly equal measure, *The New York Times* referred to the report's criticism of Israel 12 times, but only mentioned its criticism of the activists 4 times.

The Gaza "Siege"

Essential context was likewise missing from the newspaper's references to what it described as an Israeli "siege" on the Gaza Strip.

Only 6 of 37 articles mentioning Israel's border policies and naval blockade on Gaza noted Israel's stated goal of preventing weapons from entering the Gaza Strip. And even fewer reminded readers that weapons in that territory are frequently fired into Israel.

Violence

The newspaper's coverage of violence was marked by a double standard that highlighted Israeli attacks and de-emphasized Palestinian ones. Twelve headlines explicitly mentioned Palestinian fatalities; none explicitly referred to Israeli deaths, even though 14 Israelis were killed during the study period. There was also disproportionate emphasis on vandalism and non-deadly arson by radical Israeli settlers—11 articles—in comparison to Palestinian stoning attacks that resulted in deaths—4 articles.

Incitement

Least newsworthy of all, according to *The New York Times*, was the steady stream of anti-coexistence, anti-Israel and anti-Semitic rhetoric by the Palestinian leadership. Although this incitement perpetuates the conflict, only one article discussed it, and that article focused on criticism of those who chronicle the Palestinian hate rhetoric nearly as much as it did on the rhetoric itself. While Israeli actions were routinely cast as obstacles to peace, the Palestinian Authority's refusal to recognize a Jewish state was never described as an obstacle.

The Opinion Pages

On the newspaper's opinion pages, unsigned editorials consistently blamed Israel for the Palestinian-Israeli conflict. And despite assertions by *The New York Times* that "Op-Ed editors tend to look for articles that cover subjects and make arguments that have not been articulated elsewhere in the editorial space," this anti-Israel view was mirrored throughout the opinion pages, with columns and guest Op-Eds overwhelmingly in accord with *The New York Times'* editorial board.[6] Over a period of nine months, from July 2011 through March 2012, 6 of 7 editorials, 5 of 6 columns, and 4 of 7 Op-Eds about the Palestinian-Israeli conflict predominantly criticized Israel. None predominantly criticized the Palestinians.

Not only were the opinion pages unbalanced, but they heavily reflected extremist views by radical anti-Israel activists. For example, the newspaper published a column characterizing Israel's tolerance toward homosexuals as a devious ploy to conceal abuses of Palestinian human rights.

Conclusions

The newspaper's ethical code assures readers that "the goal of *The New York Times* is to cover the news as impartially as possible."[7] But Arthur Brisbane, who was *The New York Times'* public editor (ombudsman) during the study period, acknowledged that politics do, in fact, influence the newspaper's output. In his farewell column, he described a worldview of "political and cultural progressivism" that "virtually bleeds through the fabric of *The Times.*" As a result, the newspaper treats certain topics "more like causes than news subjects."[8]

This study leaves no doubt that the Palestinian-Israeli conflict is one such topic. Although the conflict is a matter of great controversy, with loud voices on all sides seeking to make their case, only one side's concerns are promoted in *The Times,* while the opposing side is marginalized. This clear pattern is far from a mere academic concern. More exposure for a viewpoint gives it more influence. By force of repetition, then, the Palestinian narrative that indicts Israel for the conflict becomes more familiar to, and as a result, more accepted by, readers of *The New York Times.*[9]

In diminishing the Israeli perspective, *The New York Times* sends another unambiguous message: Laurel Leff explained when describing the newspaper's minimization of the Holocaust that readers at the time were led to believe, "If *The New York Times* doesn't think this is an important story, why should we?"[10]

Indicting Israel aims to set the record straight on the newspaper's partisan, unprofessional coverage of the Jewish state. It provides detailed evidence that allows readers convincingly to challenge the newspaper's biased journalism and to ask, "If *The New York Times* doesn't take its own reputation for journalistic integrity seriously, why should we?"

Ricki Hollander and Gilead Ini,
Senior Research Analysts, CAMERA

---

1. Laurel Leff, *Buried by The Times: The Holocaust and America's Most Important Newspaper* (Cambridge University Press, 2005)
2. Max Frankel, "150th Anniversary: 1851-2001; Turning Away From the Holocaust," *The New York Times*, Nov. 14, 2001, http://www.nytimes.com/2001/11/14/news/150th-anniversary-1851-2001-turning-away-from-the-holocaust.html
3. Ari L. Goldman, "Telling it like it wasn't," *The Jewish Week*, Aug. 9, 2011. See also Carol B. Conaway, "Crown Heights: Politics and Press Coverage of the Race War That Wasn't," Polity 32 (Autumn 1999).

4. Ricki Hollander, "STUDY: *New York Times* Skews Israeli-Palestinian Crisis," Committee for Accuracy in Middle East Reporting in America, May 1, 2002, http://www.camera.org/index.asp?x_article=25&x_context=2.

5. See Virgil Hawkins, *Stealth Conflicts: How the World's Worst Violence is Ignored* (Hampshire, UK: Ashgate, 2008), 108-10. Hawkins notes that in *The New York Times* and other Western media corporations, "Israel received far more media coverage in a single year (2006) than the [Democratic Republic of Congo] did in all the nine years since its conflict began in 1998," even though millions of people died as a result of the latter conflict.

6. David Shipley, "And Now a Word From Op-Ed," *The New York Times*, Feb. 1, 2004, http://www.nytimes.com/2004/02/01/opinion/01SHIP.html

7. *The New York Times*, "Ethical Journalism: A Handbook of Values and Practices for the News and Editorial Departments," September 2004, http://asne.org/Portals/0/Publications/Public/newyorktimesethics.pdf.

8. Arthur S. Brisbane, "Success and Risk as *The Times* Transforms," *The New York Times*, Aug. 26, 2012.

9. In politics, repetition is tied to the theory of "priming." Professors Jon A. Krosnick and Donald R. Kinder explain that "the standards citizens use to judge a president may be substantially determined by which stories media choose to cover and, consequently, which considerations are made accessible. The more attention the news pays to a particular domain—the more frequently it is primed—the more citizens will, according to the theory, incorporate what they know about that domain into their overall judgment of the president. Hence, by calling attention to some matters while ignoring others, news media may alter the foundations of public opinion toward the president." See "Altering the Foundations of Support for the President Through Priming," *The American Political Science Review,* Vol. 84. No. 2 (June 1990), 499-500.

10. Gila Wertheimer, "Newsmakers," *Chicago Jewish Star,* June 2007.

Criticism and More Criticism: *The New York Times* Leans On Israel

Criticism and More Criticism:
The New York Times Leans On Israel

Summary

Over the course of six months in 2011, the newspaper relayed more than twice as much criticism of Israel than of the Palestinians. It is striking to find such a dramatic disproportion in coverage of a complex conflict with competing, strongly held narratives. After all, there is no shortage of critics of Hamas, the Palestinian Authority or pro-Palestinian activists. One might expect that, over time, readers of *The New York Times* would be exposed to the opposing arguments in roughly equal measure.

But between July 1 and Dec. 31, **187** passages conveyed criticism of Israel and its supporters, while only **88** passages conveyed criticism of the Palestinians and their supporters. (The criteria for classifying a passage as criticism is detailed in Appendix I: Methodology.)

Passages Criticizing Israel—Overall

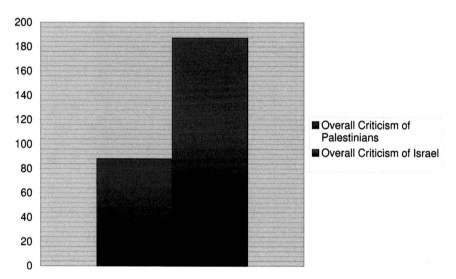

In the absence of additional information, however, these overall numbers are of limited value. They provide only a low-resolution look at how the Palestinian-Israeli conflict was reported in *The New York Times,* and do not indicate whether the discrepancy is due to journalistic bias or simply reflects dissimilar levels of popular criticism.

Perhaps more telling is the relative frequency with which the reporters themselves criticized each side.

Of the 275 passages of criticism, 30 were leveled by reporters themselves, who also faulted Israel in their own voices more than twice as often as they did the Palestinians. There were **21** statements by reporters criticizing Israel, compared to **9** criticizing the

Palestinians. This 2-to-1 ratio mirrors the disproportion in overall criticism, lending weight to the notion that *New York Times* reporters were more interested in citing statements by others that echo their own critical views of Israel than in delivering a balanced view of the conflict.

Passages Criticizing Israel—in Reporter's Voice

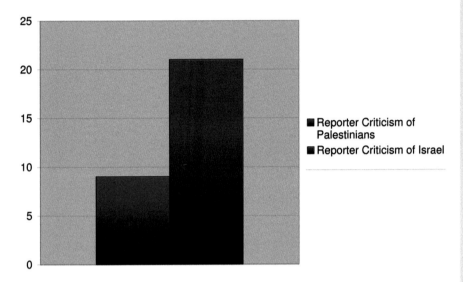

In the pages that follow, the discrepancies in the way the newspaper treats each side are discussed in much greater detail. And those pages leave no doubt that *The New York Times*—for reasons only the publisher, editors and reporters can fully explain—applies a discriminatory standard to determine which criticism, which context and which stories are considered newsworthy.

Nothing but a prejudicial view about what should be communicated to readers, for example, can reasonably account for the fact that the newspaper chose to cite mainstream Palestinians expressing their views on the peace process much more frequently than they cited mainstream Israelis opinions, as described in Chapter 1: The Peace Process.

Likewise, *The Times'* reporting on the U.N.'s Palmer Report, which criticized both Israel and pro-Palestinian activists in roughly equal measure, provides incontrovertible proof of a double standard. A newspaper covering the report in a fair and professional way would inform readers of all the report's criticisms without preference. *The New York Times* so often ignored the report's criticisms of the violent pro-Palestinian activists and so often reiterated its criticisms of the Israel that readers were exposed to the anti-Israel charges three times more often than those directed at the pro-Palestinian activists.

The newspaper's double standard thus becomes clear when focusing on specific topics such as peace talks, the Palmer Report, and other subtopics discussed in the chapters that follow. It is similarly illustrated by zooming in on specific articles.

Consider, for example, two stories published during the 6-month study period that were devoted to relaying negative characterizations of one of the two parties. In the story criticizing Israel, the critics were allowed to level accusations, including factually inaccurate statements, without challenge. But in the piece critical of the Palestinians, the critics were themselves challenged and even denigrated.

The former story centered on a fringe, anti-Israel group and its denunciation of Israeli actions and policies.[1] The article repeatedly quoted and paraphrased the group's attacks without comment or rebuttal, and included the text of an advertisement by the group published in Israel that leveled demonstrably false charges.[2] Five separate passages in the piece conveyed criticism of Israeli actions, and only one comment was vaguely critical of the accusers.

Negative charges against Palestinians, on the other hand, were treated entirely differently. A story about an Israeli group that documents examples of official Palestinian incitement to hatred and violence against Israelis included both rebuttals of the group's charges and criticism of their motives.[3] Unlike the hyperbolic, anti-Israel claims by the fringe group in the above-mentioned story, the assertions about the Palestinians were substantiated with documentation, and were echoed by mainstream Israelis and the Israeli government. While the article included eight passages of criticism against Palestinian actions, it relayed almost as much criticism—six passages—against those who documented the anti-Israel actions of Palestinians. (This is explored in greater detail in Chapter 5: Incitement.)

The double standard becomes even starker when looking at the raw numbers: The former article included 16 words of criticism of the anti-Israel group while the latter one devoted 185 words to faulting those who accused Palestinians of wrongdoing.

1. Ethan Bronner, "Where Politics Are Complex, Simple Joys At the Beach," *The New York Times*, July 27, 2011.
2. Ricki Hollander and Gilead Ini, *"The New York Times'* Bronner Advocates for Fringe Group, Censors Mainstream Concerns," Committee for Accuracy in Middle East Reporting in America, July 29, 2011, http://www.camera.org/index.asp?x_context=2&x_outlet=118&x_article=2091.
3. Isabel Kershner, "Finding Fault in the Palestinian Messages That Aren't So Public," *The New York Times*, Dec. 20, 2011.

Chapter 1

The Peace Process

The Peace Process

Summary

One of the most prominent stories related to the Palestinian-Israeli conflict during the study period was the Palestinian Authority's campaign for recognition as a state in the United Nations, also known as its attempt to achieve a "Unilateral Declaration of Independence" (UDI), and the related failure of efforts to restart peace talks.

As with most developments in the conflict, Israeli and Palestinian leaders each expressed their own perspectives on these issues, voicing strong opinions about expectations and conditions for negotiations, as well as about who is to blame for obstructing the peace process.

The topic garnered extensive *New York Times* coverage: Fifty articles, half of them carrying headlines on the topic, discussed the U.N. bid or peace negotiations. Although the rival views of the two main protagonists in the conflict form the essence of the story, the newspaper did not treat them as equally newsworthy.

Overall, the Palestinian point of view about peace talks and the UDI was relayed nearly twice as often as the Israeli point of view.

The tendency of the newspaper to emphasize the Palestinian position was apparent on a number of levels:

1. there were more articles expressing Palestinian views than those expressing Israeli views;

2. there were more total passages expressing views by Palestinians than there were expressing views by Israelis;

3. there were more unspecified third parties cited in support of the Palestinians perspective than there were in support of Israel's perspective; and

4. there were more statements in the reporter's voice backing the Palestinian position than there were backing the Israeli position.

Again and again, *New York Times* journalists editorialized, weighing in to support the Palestinian side while faulting Israeli actions for obstructing the peace process and a two-state solution. Additionally, the only unspecified third-parties cited were those expressing support of the Palestinian perspective.

Articles were further skewed by wording that consistently minimized global opposition to Palestinian unilateralism, cast aspersions on American opposition, and accepted Palestinian talking points as fact.

The Palestinian point of view about peace talks and the UDI was relayed nearly twice as often as the Israeli point of view.

Background Facts

Peace Talks

Shortly after President Barack Obama was elected president, he began to urge the Israelis and Palestinians to engage in direct negotiations. The West Bank-based Palestinian leadership demanded that Israel first freeze all settlement construction

Israelis gathered outside Benjamin Netanyahu's residence to protest his government's freeze on new construction in West Bank settlements.

and agree that the country's pre-1967 lines be the baseline for the borders of a Palestinian state. Israel rejected this, stating that negotiations should take place with everything on the table and without preconditions.

Nevertheless, in November 2009 Israeli Prime Minister Benjamin Netanyahu risked domestic opposition by agreeing to an unprecedented 10-month moratorium on building in the West Bank. Palestinian President Mahmoud Abbas dismissed this gesture as inadequate because it did not include a freeze on construction in eastern Jerusalem, which Israel considers its sovereign territory and Palestinians consider occupied land. Abbas continued to reject Netanyahu's entreaties that he rejoin the negotiating process without preconditions, but under intense pressure from the U.S. and European countries he eventually agreed to engage in so-called proximity talks—shuttle diplomacy by special U.S. envoy George Mitchell.

Finally, on September 2, 2010, only a few weeks before Israel's 10-month settlement moratorium was slated to end, the Palestinian Authority (PA) yielded to American calls to join Israel at the negotiating table. When the moratorium terminated on September 26, Abbas abandoned negotiations and refused to resume them unless Israel extended its settlement freeze. The Israeli prime minister, for his part, announced his readiness to impose another settlement freeze provided the Palestinians accept Israel as a Jewish state. According to Israel, Palestinian recognition of the Jewish right to self-determination parallels Israeli recognition of a Palestinian right to self-determination and lies at the heart of a mutual commitment to a two-state solution. Any agreement not predicated upon such acceptance therefore would be seen by Israel as evidence of Palestinian unwillingness to end the conflict.[1]

The PA leader, however, refused to grant Israel such recognition. Abbas reiterated this position in an October 2011 interview on Egyptian TV when he stated, "I've said it before, and I'll say it again: I will never recognize the Jewishness of the state, or a 'Jewish state.'"[2]

Throughout the study period, Israel continued to urge the Palestinian leadership to return to the negotiating table for peace talks without preconditions.[3] The Palestinians continuously refused.

Statements made by both sides in October 2011 exemplified their respective points of view. Netanyahu's spokesman Mark Regev urged the Palestinians to abandon their unilateral bid for statehood:

> Israel welcomes the Quartet's call for direct negotiations between the parties without preconditions, as called for by both President Obama and Prime Minister Netanyahu. While Israel has some concerns, it will raise them at the appropriate time. Israel calls on the Palestinian Authority to do the same and to enter into direct negotiations without delay.[4]

Palestinian negotiator Nabil Shaath was quoted by German wire service Deutsche Presse-Agentur repeating his side's conditions:

> "Our demands are very clear and they will not change for any reason," said Shaath, who is also a leading member in President Mahmoud Abbas' Fatah movement. Unless Israel complies with these conditions, he said, "we will not return to negotiations. There is just no use from them."[5]

Unilateral Declaration of Independence (UDI)

Instead of re-entering negotiations, the Palestinian Authority focused its attention on promoting its Unilateral Declaration of Independence at the United Nations. It lobbied world leaders and international institutions to recognize Palestine as a state even in the absence of a peace agreement with Israel, and announced that it would bring its request to the United Nations for a vote to endorse the Palestinian demand.

Some countries, especially in Latin America, responded to PA requests by recognizing a state of Palestine. But many leaders in the US and Europe made clear that they supported direct negotiations and were opposed to unilateral Palestinian moves at the United Nations.[6]

In November 2011, the Palestinians gained membership in UNESCO, but shortly thereafter learned that the U.N. Security Council, including the United States, Colombia and each of the five European countries on the Council, would not be supporting their unilateralist bid.[7]

Palestinian leaders continued to lobby for membership in the United Nations, and threatened to renew their UDI push in the future.

Mahmoud Abbas shows a letter requesting U.N. membership for the Palestinians, a unilateral move he pursued outside the framework of negotiations with Israel.

Coverage by the Numbers

- 50 articles during the study period relayed points of view on the peace process or UDI. Of those, **5** articles, or 10 percent, presented only Israeli perspectives. Three times as many —**18** articles, or 36 percent—presented only Palestinian perspectives.

- Overall, there were nearly twice as many passages presenting a Palestinian position on the UDI or peace process as those presenting an Israeli perspective.

106 passages presented a Palestinian view on the topic. **60** passages presented an Israeli view.

These passages fell into three general categories:

1. views or statements attributed to Israelis or Palestinians;

2. views or statements attributed to unspecified third parties; and

3. unattributed statements in the reporter's voice endorsing the position of one side or the other.

In every one of these categories, the Palestinian view predominated.

- The newspaper published **81** passages citing only Palestinians expressing a position on the peace process, compared to **50** passages citing only Israelis expressing a position. Another **8** passages cited both Israelis and Palestinians.

Articles Relaying Points of View on Peace Process and UDI

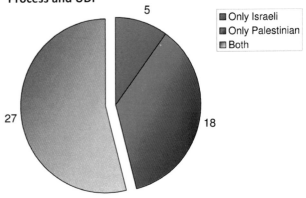

Number of Passages Expressing a Party's Point of View on Peace Process or UDI

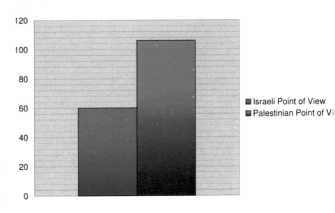

For example:

Attributed to Palestinians

> The Palestinians say negotiations are pointless because they believe Israel has no desire to see a Palestinian state come into being.[8] (Aug. 30, 2011)

Attributed to Israelis

> Israel has argued that Palestinian pursuit of statehood membership in the United Nations and its joining forces with Hamas, which has not renounced violence or recognized Israel, amount to abrogation of the Oslo accords, freeing Israel to react accordingly.[9] (Dec. 1, 2011)

Attributed to Both

> Each side says that it wants direct talks and peace but that the other side does not.[10] (Sept. 6, 2011)

• Articles also cited unspecified third parties—described as "supporters," "advocates" or "analysts"— that reinforced one side's stance. There were **4** such statements reinforcing the Palestinian point of view versus **0** reinforcing the Israeli point of view. Although there are certainly supporters and analysts who share Israel's perspective, journalists chose not to cite their views.

An example of a view attributed to an unspecified third party includes:

> Supporters contend it is high time to shift the negotiations out of the State Department basement into the glare of an international forum ...[11] (Sept. 19, 2011)

• Not only did *New York Times* reporters cite others expressing views on the peace process, they also weighed in with their own voices. Such editorializing appeared almost exclusively in support of Palestinian positions, lending them authority by presenting them as fact. In **12** instances, reporters presented the Palestinian view as fact. For example, Israel was faulted, in the reporter's voice, for "obstructing" peace, a viewpoint frequently put forth by Palestinians and their supporters but rejected by Israel and its supporters:

> [The Israelis] are holding land widely considered Palestinian by right, obstructing a two-state solution.[12] (Sept. 24, 2011)

By contrast, reporters presented Israeli views as fact only **2** times. Once was in a passage in which the reporter relayed both sides' views, stating that as a result of actions by Israelis and Palestinians, "recent efforts to bring the sides back to the negotiating table appeared to be moving in reverse."[13] The other passage presented as fact that Israel "fears militant groups and missiles would penetrate" a future Palestinian state "unless Israel controls its borders."[14]

Number of Passages in Which a Reporter Editorializes a Point of View on Peace Process or UDI

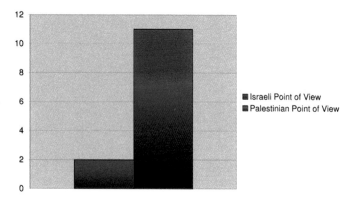

■ Israeli Point of View
■ Palestinian Point of View

Editorializing

Understating Opposition to the UDI

In the period leading up to the Palestinians' formal U.N. membership request, *The New York Times* increased the number of articles published about the controversial issue, many of which focused primarily on Palestinian frustrations and their stated justification for going to the United Nations.

The newspaper repeatedly minimized international opposition to the unilateral Palestinian move by suggesting that the only opponents were the U.S. and Israel. For example, reporter Neil MacFarquhar wrote:

Opponents, essentially Israel and the United States, condemned the idea as an ineffective "shortcut" that would not budge the deadlocked peace negotiations.[15] (July 27, 2011)

Other stories contributed to this misconception by likewise referring only to "Israel and the United States" taking issue with the unilateral Palestinian actions:

"Israel and the United States have urged the Palestinian Authority not to seek the United Nations vote, and to engage instead in direct negotiations with Israel."[16] (Aug. 30, 2011)

"Membership for Palestine was opposed by both the United States and Israel because it was seen as part of the Palestinian quest for international recognition as a state without a negotiated agreement."[17] (Nov. 9, 2011)

"Israel and the United States have tried to stop the showdown altogether, warning of dire consequences and insisting that the only way to resolve the Israeli-Palestinian conflict is through direct negotiations."[18] (Sept. 15, 2011)

"Internationally, however, the United States and Israel appeared increasingly isolated."[19] (Sept. 14, 2011)

Other media outlets at the time, however, noted that Canada, the Czech Republic and the Netherlands were among those opposed to the bid, and that additional world powers were on the fence.[20] On rare occasion, even *The New York Times* itself acknowledged that "the major countries [in Europe] appear divided, with Germany and Italy rejecting the Palestinian campaign...."[21] Indeed, the Palestinians ultimately were unable to convince the needed 9 of 15 countries on the U.N. Security Council to back the bid and bring the matter to a vote.[22]

Disparaging American Opposition

Not only did the newspaper deceptively describe opposition to the Palestinian moves as being limited to the United States and Israel, it also editorialized, in news stories, against the U.S. position.

One of Abbas's talking points in defense of his UDI bid was to compare it to the ongoing uprisings against authoritarian Arab leaders—events known collectively as the Arab Spring.[23] Despite dramatic differences between the two issues, as a public relations move Abbas's attempt to link them made sense.[24] The Arab Spring uprisings were widely regarded in a positive light, and Abbas was actively seeking such international support for his unilateral statehood moves.[25]

A Sept. 24 article in *The Times* showed Abbas drawing the analogy during a speech at the U.N.:

Connecting his statehood request with the Arab uprisings, he said, "The time has come also for the Palestinian spring, the time for independence."[26]

It was not only Abbas, though, who drew the questionable connection. Even before the above passage was published, *New York Times* reporters repeatedly evoked the UDI bid as being self-evidently analogous to anti-authoritarian movements in Arab

By opining that the American preference for unconditional negotiations rather than unilateral moves amounts to standing in the way of the Arab democracy movement, *The Times* flatly expressed a political position in its news pages.

states, editorializing that it would be uncomfortable, troubling or even hypocritical for the United States to oppose the former while supporting the latter.

In one story, reporter Jennifer Steinhaur wrote of the inherent discomfort that must be associated with the American position:

> Now the Palestinians are weighing a request to the United Nations Security Council to support a bid for statehood, leaving Washington in the uncomfortable position of blocking such a unilateral move while supporting democracy movements in other Arab nations.[27] (Aug. 16, 2011)

Another article, by Helene Cooper and Neil MacFarquhar, described the "trouble" with the American position, and made sure to underscore why it could be seen as hypocritical:

> The trouble for Mr. Obama, though, is that even as he was publicly proclaiming his backing at the United Nations for a new Libyan state, American officials were working furiously behind the scenes to make sure the United Nations did not bestow a similar recognition on a Palestinian state. ...

> Mr. Obama is scheduled to speak before the General Assembly on Wednesday morning, where he will have to address the Palestinian issue. It is a high-wire act for him, and officials privately acknowledge that the president risks appearing hypocritical.

> "Today the world is saying, in one unmistakable voice, 'We will stand with you as you seize this moment of promise; as you reach for the freedom, the dignity and the opportunity you deserve,'" he said Tuesday. **But he was talking about Libyans, not Palestinians.**[28] (Sept. 21, 2011)

The same authors were more direct in a report published the following day:

> President Obama declared his opposition to the Palestinian Authority's bid for statehood through the Security Council on Wednesday, throwing the weight of the United States directly in the path of the Arab democracy movement even as he hailed what he called the democratic aspirations that have taken hold throughout the Middle East and North Africa.[29] (Sept. 22, 2011)

By opining that the American preference for unconditional negotiations over unilateral moves stands in the way of the Arab democracy movement, *The Times* flatly expressed a political position in its news pages, violating journalistic guidelines calling on reporters to "distinguish between advocacy and news reporting."[30]

Palestinian Feelings vs. Israeli Claims

Several news stories presented Palestinian talking points about the controversy as fact. For example, in a Sept. 22, 2011 story Neil MacFarqhar and Ethan Bronner purported to know the inner motivations of Palestinian president Mahmoud Abbas:

> Fruitless negotiations with Israel **made [Abbas] feel as if he had little choice—and little to lose**—by taking his case to the sympathetic world forum.

And later in the article:

> Mr. Netanyahu ultimately pulled the plug on those talks, **leaving Mr. Abbas a sense of having no alternatives.**[31]

Did Abbas really feel that he had "little choice," and did he actually sense that he had "no alternatives" to his U.N. bid? Or was that simply how his political advisors suggested he frame the unilateral move?

By contrast, the newspaper generally, and appropriately, relayed Israeli talking points as stated positions, not feelings. For example, while Abbas was described as "feeling" and "sensing," reporters stuck to the facts when describing Israel or its leaders as "saying," "arguing" or taking a "position":

> "**Israel says** that the Palestinians have made a strategic decision to seek recognition of an outline of a state without the give and take of negotiations and that last time they waited nine months before agreeing to start talks."[32] (Oct. 3 2011)

> "For his part, **Mr. Netanyahu said** direct negotiations were the only option."[33] (Sept. 6, 2011)

> "**Israeli officials argue** that a resolution recognizing a Palestinian state could complicate the prospect of talks beyond salvation."[34] (Sept. 6, 2011)

> "The basic **Israeli position ... is** that the two sides have to negotiate the main six outstanding issues including borders, the status of Jerusalem and the return of refugees."[35] (July 27, 2011)

Two consecutive passages in one article by Ethan Bronner demonstrated the newspaper's tendency to describe Israeli statements as claims and Palestinian positions as feelings. The first paragraph described an incontrovertible fact as nothing more than an Israeli claim: Benjamin Netanyahu *said* Israel had frozen construction in settlements and that the Palestinians only agreed to negotiations when the freeze was set to expire. The subsequent paragraph stated, as fact, a Palestinian claim that they were "despairing" of negotiations and "hoping" that going to the U.N. would alleviate their problem:

> Prime Minister Benjamin Netanyahu of Israel has himself consistently rejected a settlement freeze, **saying** that he had tried one for 10 months and that the Palestinians came to negotiate only after nine of those months had elapsed.

> The Palestinians, **despairing** of the negotiation process, have approached the United Nations in hopes of improving their position.[36] (Sept. 26, 2011)

Other times, the newspaper went even further, describing Israeli assertions not as feelings, and not even as stated positions, but rather as spin:

> Mr. Netanyahu's office **seemed eager to sound open** to renewing talks even after Mr. Abbas presents his membership request letter to the United Nations."[37] (Sept. 18, 2011)

Again, it is worth comparing this skeptical description of Israeli political positioning to a passage published a week earlier describing with certainty a Palestinian politician's inner feelings:

> Two consecutive passages in one article by Ethan Bronner demonstrates the newspaper's tendency to describe Israeli statements as claims and Palestinian positions as feelings.

When Mr. Netanyahu refused to extend a moratorium on construction, **Mr. Abbas felt let down.**[38] (Sept. 10, 2011)

One article in particular, "Palestinians Turn to U.N., Where Partition Began" by Neil MacFarquhar, exemplifies *The Times'* emphasis on the Palestinian perspective. As in the examples above, the article presented a Palestinian talking point as fact, reporting that

> The Palestinians see the membership application as a last-ditch attempt to preserve the two-state solution in the face of ever-encroaching Israeli settlements, as well as a desperate move to shake up the negotiations that they feel have achieved little after 20 years of American oversight.[39] (Sept. 19, 2011)

The story did not similarly describe how the Israelis "see the membership application," nor did it provide Israel's perspective on how to preserve the two-state solution. Israelis have argued that Palestinian encouragement of terrorism and its rejection of coexistence with a Jewish state are what prevent peace, but nowhere did the article relay Israel's concerns.

Instead, the article repeatedly cited supporters of the controversial Palestinian U.N. campaign. The above-quoted passage explained how Palestinians see the application. A subsequent passage quoted a former U.N. official expressing support for the plan. Another featured unnamed Palestinian "supporters" declaring what "they believe." Next, some unidentified "analysts" argued that the plan "is the only leverage left to the Palestinians." (As indicated in the Coverage by the Numbers section, no other anonymous analysts who might have disagreed with this assessment were given a voice, although such analysts certainly exist.[40])

Yet again, the article informed readers what "Palestinians believe," and another passage cited former Palestinian official Rashid Khalidi justifying the Palestinian position.

Mahmoud Abbas listens as Barack Obama speaks during the Sept. 11, 2011 meeting of the General Assembly at the U.N. headquarters.

Only once, near the end of the story and after dwelling at length on the views of Palestinians, their supporters and sympathetic analysts, did the story finally allude to an Israeli position by stating that Israel "accuses" the Palestinians of avoiding negotiations.

However, the reporter quickly turned back to the Palestinian point of view, underscoring in his own voice that the Palestinian move was meant to overcome "right-wing domestic constraints in the United States and Israel that have helped stall negotiations for at least 18 months." Thus, MacFarquhar reported as fact Israel's alleged responsibility for stalled negotiations, while Palestinian responsibility was presented only as an "accusation" by Israel. And the article ended with a quote stating that the U.N. bid was driven by Palestinian desperation.

An associated photo caption reiterated the theme of the article: "Palestinians seek to preserve the two-state solution in the face of encroaching Israeli settlements like this one in the West Bank." In other words, readers were informed, on the news pages, that Israel was undermining a two-state solution, while the Palestinian UDI campaign was meant to save it.

Clearly, Israeli views and concerns were not considered important. Not a word was said about Abbas's refusal to engage in direct negotiations, his preconditions, or his refusal to recognize the legitimacy of the Jewish state. The article read more like a promotion of the Palestinian position than a straightforward news article presenting the facts.

An Obstacle to Peace

Meanwhile, the few articles that did refer to Palestinian refusal to accept the Jewish state—a position Israelis view as antithetical to the essence of a mutual commitment to a two-state solution—did not cast it as an obstacle to peace. Instead, it was presented as an understandable or even justifiable position. For example:

> The Palestinians have never acceded to a formal recognition of Israel as a Jewish state, in deference at least in part to the Palestinians who live in Israel.[41] (Sept. 4, 2011)

The passage accepted as self-evident truth that Jewish national self-determination inherently harms the country's minorities. And it ignored the alternative view that Palestinian leaders' rejection of a Jewish state exemplifies their opposition per se to the very principle of two states for two people.

Not once during the study period did The New York Times cite the Israeli prime minister or officials expressing their opinion that a main obstacle to ending Palestinian-Israeli conflict is the Palestinian refusal to accept a Jewish state in the region. Reporters did not quote, for example, Netanyahu's Sept. 23, 2011 statement at the U.N. that

> The core of the conflict is not the settlements. The settlements are a result of the conflict. ... But the core of the conflict has always been and unfortunately remains the refusal of the Palestinians to recognize a Jewish state in any border.[42]

Nor did they ever quote Israel officials explaining why Palestinian refusal to acknowledge a Jewish state is viewed as the central obstacle to ending the conflict.[43] Instead, the newspaper provided multiple passages in which Israel was faulted, both

Readers were informed, on the news pages, that Israel was undermining a two-state solution, while the Palestinian UDI campaign was meant to save it.

During the study period, readers of The New York Times were exposed to Palestinian views about a central controversy in the conflict—the peace process and the UDI—nearly twice as often as they were exposed to Israeli views on the subject. This discrepancy is journalistically indefensible.

in the voice of Palestinian officials and in the reporter's own voice, for obstructing a two-state solution. For example,

> "They are holding land widely considered Palestinian by right, obstructing a two-state solution."[44] (Sept. 24, 2011)

> "The Palestinians, arguing that ongoing settlement activity by Israel is gradually erasing the prospects for a two-state solution based on the 1967 borders, say that membership would solidify the effort toward such a resolution."[45] (July 27, 2011)

> "... Saeb Erekat, who was in Paris with President Mahmoud Abbas of the Palestinian Authority, was quoted by Agence France-Presse as saying it proved ''the Israeli government wants to destroy the peace process and the two-state solution."[46] (Oct. 15, 2011)

Conclusion

During the study period, readers of *The New York Times* were exposed to Palestinian views about a central controversy in the conflict—the peace process and the UDI—nearly twice as often as they were exposed to Israeli views on the subject. This discrepancy is journalistically indefensible. Had there been a consistent standard, both points of view would have been considered equally newsworthy and, over time, would have been represented in roughly equal measure. Because this was not the portrayal offered, readers were left with greater exposure to, and understanding of, Palestinian perspectives on the issues.

Adding to the preponderance of Palestinian speakers on the topic were reporters' own editorializing comments on the issue and their citations of generic "supporters," "advocates," and "analysts" backing only one side.

In news reports, journalists presented in their own voice the opinion that Israel, and not the Palestinians, is obstructing peace. They often accepted as fact Palestinian talking points about their motivations and feelings, while describing similar Israeli talking points as attributed claims.

To expose readers disproportionately to one party's perspective over another's in a deeply contentious debate is an approach to purveying information that is the hallmark of advocacy journalism rather than objective news reporting.

1. Tal Becker, executive summary to *The Claim for Recognition of Israel as a Jewish State: A Reassessment* (Washington, D.C., The Washington Institute for Near East Policy, 2011),
2. Mahmoud Abbas, Oct. 23, 2011, Dream 2 TV (Egypt); recorded and translated by MEMRI, http://www.memritv.org/clip/en/3163.htm.
3. Ariel Zirulnick, "What are the Israeli-Palestinian peace talk preconditions?," *Christian Science Monitor,* Oct. 26, 2011.
4. "Israel welcomes Quartet call for direct negotiations," Israel Ministry of Foreign Affairs, Oct. 2, 2011, http://www.mfa.gov.il/MFA/Government/Communiques/2011/Israel_welcomes_Quartet_call_direct_negotiations_2-Oct-2011.
5. "No expectations from Quartet meetings, Palestinians say," Deutsche Presse-Agentur, October 26, 2011.

6. "Fact Sheet: Palestinian Unilateral Declaration of Independence," Jewish Virtual Library, Sept. 23, 2011, http://www.jewishvirtuallibrary.org/jsource/talking/81_PalestinianUDI.html.
7. Flavia Krause-Jackson, "Palestinians Weigh U.N. Vote on Membership After Setback," Bloomberg, November 14, 2011.
8. Ethan Bronner, "Palestinian Man Injures 8 at Israeli Club, Police Say," Aug. 30, 2011.
9. Ethan Bronner, "Palestinians To Receive Payments, Israel Says," Dec. 1, 2011.
10. Ethan Bronner, "Abbas Affirms Palestinian Bid for U.N. Membership," Sept. 6, 2011.
11. Neil MacFarquhar, "Palestinians Turn To U.N., Where Partition Began," Sept. 19, 2011.
12. Ethan Bronner, "Amid Statehood Bid, Tensions Simmer in West Bank," Sept. 24, 2011.
13. Isabel Kershner, "Israel Plans to Speed Up Settlement Growth," Nov. 2, 2011.
14. Ethan Bronner and Isabel Kershner, "Palestinians Set Bid for U.N. Seat; A Clash with U.S.," Sept. 17, 2011.
15. Neil MacFarquhar, "Security Council Debate Offers Preview of Palestinian Bid," July 27, 2011.
16. Bronner, "Palestinian Man Injures 8 at Israeli Club, Police Say," Aug. 30, 2011.
17. Isabel Kershner, "In Overheard Comments, Sarkozy Calls Netanyahu a 'Liar,'" Nov. 9, 2011.
18. Isabel Kershner, "Palestinians Say a U.N. Gamble on Statehood Is Worth the Risks," Sept. 15, 2011.
19. Steven Lee Myers and David D. Kirkpatrick, "U.S. Scrambles to Avert Palestinian Vote at U.N.," Sept. 14, 2011.
20. Alina Wolfe Murray and Aron Heller, "Israel's prime minister gets backing from Romania," Associated Press, July 6, 2011; Ronen Medzini, "Palestinian U.N. bid: Israel's battle for Europe," Ynet News, http://www.ynetnews.com/articles/0,7340,L-4074239,00.html.
21. Mark Landler, "As U.S. Steps Back, Europe Takes Bigger Role in Mideast Peace Push," July 21, 2011. This piece was published days before the newspaper cast opponents of the UDI as amounting to "essentially Israel and the United States."
22. Chris McGreal, "UN vote on Palestinian state put off amid lack of support," The Guardian (UK), Nov. 11, 2011, http://www.guardian.co.uk/world/2011/nov/11/united-nations-delays-palestinian-statehood-vote.
23. "Abbas urges Europe: Support Palestinian spring," Ma'an News, Oct. 6, 2011, http://www.maannews.net/eng/ViewDetails.aspx?ID=426646.
24. Most broadly, the Arab Spring uprisings were intranational revolts in states long ruled by autocratic leaders. The Palestinian UDI was undertaken by an authority that recently was offered, and rejected, statehood as part of a peace agreement. Its intent was to avoid negotiations or otherwise to pressure Israel into making concessions prior to negotiations.
25. "Global poll reveals widespread support for Arab Spring protest," BBC World Service Publicity, last modified Dec. 12, 2011.
26. Neil MacFarquhar and Steven Lee Myers, "As Palestinians seek U.N. Entry, a push for talks," Sept. 24, 2011.
27. "A Recess Destination with Bipartisan Support: Israel and the West Bank," Aug. 16, 2011.
28. "Obama Praises Libya's Post-Revolution Leaders at the United Nations," Sept. 21, 2011.
29. "Obama says Palestinians are using wrong forum," Sept. 22, 2011.
30. Society of Professional Journalists Code of Ethics.
31. "Taking a Stand, and Shedding Arafat's Shadow," September 22, 2011.
32. Isabel Kershner, "Israel Accepts New Peace Talks, but Impasse Remains on Terms," October 3, 2011.
33. Bronner, "Abbas Affirms."
34. Ibid.
35. MacFarquhar, "Security Council Debate."
36. "Palestinians Roll Out Hero's Welcome for Abbas," Sept. 26, 2011.
37. Ethan Bronner and Isabel Kershner, "Palestinians See U.N. Appeal as Most Viable Option," Sept. 18, 2011.
38. Mark Landler, "Obama and Abbas: From Speed Dial to Not Talking," Sept. 10, 2011.
39. "Palestinians Turn To U.N."
40. For example, Fouad Ajami of Johns Hopkins' School of Advanced International Studies and the Hoover Institution argued that a Palestinian victory at the U.N. "would be hollow" because for the Palestinians "there can be no escape from negotiations with Israel" (Fouad Ajami, "The U.N. Can't Deliver a Palestinian State," The Wall Street Journal, June 1, 2011). Former U.S. peace negotiator Aaron David Miller stated that the Palestinian UDI bid "takes dumb to a new level" (Aaron David Miller, "The Palestinians' mistake in seeking statehood from the U.N.," The Washington Post, April 14, 2011).
41. Steven Lee Myers and Mark Landler, "U.S. Is Appealing To Palestinians To Stall U.N. Vote," September 4, 2011.
42. Benjamin Netanyahu, address to the U.N. General Assembly, Sept. 23, 2011, http://unispal.un.org/UNISPAL.NSF/0/93AFB927919E10588525793500537B16.
43. See, e.g., Yosef Kuperwasser and Shalom Lipner, "The Problem Is Palestinian Rejectionism," Foreign

Affairs, Nov.-Dec. 2011; Ron Prosor, "Remarks by Israeli Ambassador to the UK Ron Prosor to the U.N. General Assembly," Nov. 29, 2011, http://www.mfa.gov.il/ MFA/Foreign+Relations/Israel+and+the+UN/Speeches+-+statements/Amb_Prosor_ addresses_UNGA_29-Nov-2011.htm.

44. Bronner, "Amid Statehood Bid."
45. MacFarquhar, "Security Council Debate."
46. Rick Gladstone, "Israel Plans to Build More Housing in East Jerusalem," Oct. 15, 2011.

Chapter 2

Amnesia on a Turkish Ship

Amnesia on a Turkish Ship

Summary

A frequently revisited topic during the study period was the deterioration of relations between Turkey and Israel. This was blamed primarily on an incident in 2010 in which Israeli attempts to bar a Turkish ship, the *Mavi Marmara,* from illegally entering the Gaza Strip resulted in the deaths of Turkish citizens. A United Nations review of the event, commonly known as the Palmer Report, was released during the period of the study, bringing fresh attention to the controversial incident.

All of *The New York Times'* references to the *Mavi Marmara* incident were examined, including coverage of the Palmer Report. The newspaper's treatment of the event exemplified its overall distortion of the news by depriving readers of crucial context and by selectively relaying criticism.

Nearly 80 percent of articles that mentioned Israel's use of force aboard the ship completely ignored the corresponding events—the violent attacks by anti-Israel activists on board that precipitated Israel's response. Moreover, and in line with *The New York Times'* general overemphasis on criticism of Israel, the newspaper included four times as much criticism of Israel's actions as it did criticism of the activists' violence. And while the U.N. report criticized both the violent passengers and the Israeli response, the newspaper cited the report's criticism of Israel three times more often than it cited the report's criticism of the activists.

Background Facts

In May 2010, Israeli naval commandos boarded the *Mavi Marmara*, a passenger ship owned by a Turkish Islamist group, as it attempted to break the naval blockade on the Gaza Strip. As the commandos landed on the deck, they were violently attacked by passengers, who stabbed, beat and injured several of the Israelis. Two commandos were reportedly shot and three were captured by passengers and taken below deck; nine activists were killed in the Israeli counterattack.[1]

Israeli-Turkish relations, which had already significantly soured after Recep Tayyip Erdogan rose to power in Turkey, were further damaged by the incident.[2]

In September 2011, a report on the incident commissioned by U.N. Secretary General Ban Ki-moon was published. It was formally titled *The United Nations' Report of the Secretary-General's Panel of Inquiry on the 31 May 2010 Flotilla Incident* and more commonly known as the Palmer Report.

The report concluded that Israel's blockade was a legal and legitimate security measure; that the "the flotilla acted recklessly" and that there are "serious questions about the conduct, true nature and objectives of the flotilla organizers"; that the timing and method of Israel's interception was "excessive and unreasonable"; that the Israeli personnel had to use force for their protection because they faced significant and organized violence; that the loss of life resulting from Israel's use of force was unacceptable; and that captured Israeli soldiers and passengers were mistreated.[3]

> **Nearly 80 percent of articles that mentioned Israel's use of force aboard the ship completely ignored the corresponding events—the violent attacks by anti-Israel activists on board that precipitated Israel's response.**

Coverage by the Numbers

Context

- Of **37** articles that referenced Israel's use of force on the *Mavi Marmara*, only **8** mentioned the activists' violence.

That is, nearly 80 percent of those articles omitted context for Israel's resort to force, at best suggesting it occurred in a vacuum and, at worst, framing it as a gratuitous attack on peaceful civilians.

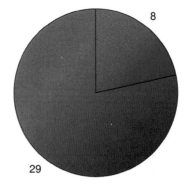

Articles Referencing Israeli Use of Force on *Mavi Mamara*

■ Mentioned Activist Violence
■ Ignored Activist Violence

The Sept. 27, 2011 story "Turkish Paper Lists Israelis It Says Were in Flotilla Raid" focused entirely, as the headline indicates, on the *Marmara* incident. Paragraph after paragraph referred to "the raid," "the death of nine passengers" and Turkish threats of "legal action."[4] But like 28 other *New York Times* stories during the study period that referred to violence aboard the ship, there was not even the briefest mention that Israel's soldiers were attacked.

A September 12, 2011 story touching on Israel's use of force left out context not only for why the boarding of the ship turned violent, but even for why there was a raid at all. The article referred to Turkish anger over "a raid that killed nine people last year on a Turkish protest ship bound for Gaza," yet avoided mentioning the furious and violent attack by the passengers, and avoided noting that the ship was attempting to illegally break a naval blockade.[5]

Even among the few stories that did acknowledge the activists' violence, not all did so in a straightforward manner. Despite the fact that the activists' attacks are well-documented on video, and although *Times* stories published prior to the study period reported frankly on the passengers' assaults on Israeli soldiers, an article during the study period cast the violence as nothing more than an Israeli "account"—in other words, an allegation by Israel that may or may not be true. (See details below.) Another obscured the sequence of activist attack and Israeli counterattack, and the degree of violence against Israel, by stating only that the activists were killed after "scuffles ensued."[6]

In all, then, only 6 stories of the 37 included straightforward references to the activists' violence. Of those, 4 references were attributed to the Palmer Report, leaving only 2 stories in which violence by the activists was presented forthrightly, as fact, in the reporter's voice. By contrast, nearly all references to the killing of activists were made in the reporter's authoritative voice.

Criticism

- **20** passages conveyed criticism of Israel's actions relating to the *Mavi Marmara* incident. By contrast, only **5** passages conveyed criticism of the activists.

There was intense and loud criticism of the activists by Israel, its citizens, and its supporters that reporters could have cited, but they simply chose not to, presenting a 4:1 disproportion in criticism of Israel.

- The newspaper's tendency to focus on criticism of Israel was even more clearly demonstrated by its reporting of the U.N. report about the incident. The Palmer Report criticized both the activists and the Israelis. And it criticized the sides roughly in equal measure—two points in the report's summary criticized the flotilla passengers and three points criticized Israel.[7] Yet the newspaper reported on the criticism of Israel 3 times as often. *The New York Times* repeated the report's criticism of Israel **12** separate times, but referenced its criticism of the activists only **4** times.

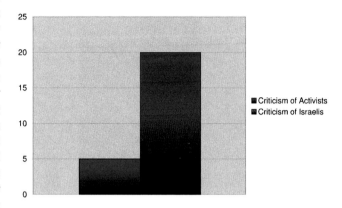

All Passages Criticizing *Marmara* Parties

In several articles, the report's criticism of Israel was deemed newsworthy while its criticism of the activists was ignored completely. For example, a Sept. 6, 2011 article by Ethan Bronner and Sebnem Arsu stated that "the report said the Israeli forces reacted to the attack in a way that was both excessive and unreasonable" without even hinting at the fact that the report also raised "serious questions about the conduct, true nature and objectives of the flotilla organizers" or that it criticized passengers for having "captured, mistreated, and placed at risk" Israeli commandos.[8]

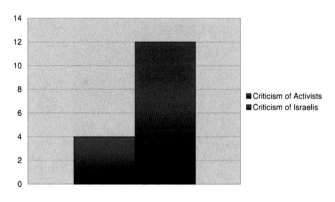

Passages Citing Palmer Report Criticism of Marmara Parties

Editorializing

A front page article published on Sept. 2 is illustrative of *The New York Times'* one-sided reporting about the Palmer Report.

The piece, by Neil MacFarquhar and Ethan Bronner, broke the story of the U.N.

findings. While the newspaper could easily have run a headline that relayed the U.N.'s criticism evenhandedly, it instead chose a title that focused solely on Israel and ignored the report's criticism of the activists: "U.N. Faults Israel On Flotilla Raid, Not On Blockade." (A more fair and factual alternative might have been "U.N. Faults Both Passengers and Israel On Flotilla Raid.")

The text of the piece was similarly skewed. The report's criticism of Israel was featured in each of the first two paragraphs. Its criticism of the flotilla activists and organizers, however, did not appear until deep inside the story after the jump, diminishing its importance in the account and its likelihood of being read.

The third paragraph stated that both sides criticized the report's conclusions, but the article only spelled out Turkey's objections, and never explained those expressed by Israel.

Subsequent paragraphs meandered through smaller details—the "no comment" expressed by the Turkish and Israeli foreign ministries; negotiations by the sides about stopping publication of the report; debates about an Israeli apology; additional Turkish complaints about the report; and the composition of the U.N. fact-finding—all the while failing to mention that the report criticized the violent *Mavi Marmara* passengers.

It was only in the 14th paragraph, more than halfway through the story, that some of the report's criticism of the activists and organizers, which were among the report's major findings, were finally noted. The story never reported on the report's criticism that passengers "mistreated" captured Israeli soldiers, though it *twice* mentioned its criticisms about Israeli mistreatment of passengers.[9]

A story published the following day again mentioned the Palmer Report. And again, each of the report's criticisms of Israel was mentioned while its criticisms of the flotilla organizers and the passengers who mistreated captured Israeli soldiers were ignored completely.[10]

> **The Palmer Report's criticism of Israel was featured in each of the first two paragraphs. Its criticism of the flotilla activists and organizers, however, did not appear until deep inside the story after the jump.**

Activist Violence as an Israeli "Account"

Of the eight articles that bothered to mention activists' violence, one, an article by Isabel Kershner, did so by describing the attacks as nothing more than a claim by Israel. It stated:

> By Israel's account, the Israeli soldiers met with violent resistance.[11] (Aug. 18, 2011)

Of course, it was not only in "Israel's account" that the soldiers were savagely attacked. Widely publicized video footage, shot from multiple angles, shows clearly the Israelis being descended upon and pummeled with metal bars and even knives as they boarded the ship, with one being beaten and hurled off a deck.[12]

The accounts of other observers coincided with the video evidence. The attack on the Israeli soldiers began, as retired British Marine Officer Peter Cook acknowledged on British television, as the first Israeli soldier lowered himself onto the ship.[13]

This was also the account of Turkish journalist Sefik Dinç, a passenger on the *Mavi*

A Gaza flotilla "activist" beats an Israeli soldier aboard the Mavi Marmara, caught on video.

Marmara and witness to the violence. He acknowledged that the soldiers were "met with resistance" when they boarded.[14]

Mohmut Koskun, another Turkish passenger describing the attack on the Israeli soldiers, said that passengers "ran at them without pause or hesitation." Notably, Koskun's description of events was published in *The New York Times* just after the *Marmara* incident occurred, one year before the study period.[15]

Indeed, in the same article in which Koskun was quoted, the reporters themselves noted that "when three Israeli commandos slid down ropes out of helicopters to take over the ship, a crowd set upon them. ... One soldier was stabbed and two were beaten."

A *Times* story that twice mentioned the U.N. report's criticism that Israel mistreated flotilla passengers never cited the same report's finding that passengers mistreated captured Israeli soldiers.

Bizarrely, it was the same *New York Times* reporter who during the study period described the violence as an Israeli "account" who had eight months earlier accurately described the reality of the violence. In a January 2011 story, Isabel Kershner acknowledged that "video images released at the time showed Israeli commandos being set upon as they rappelled from helicopters onto the ship's deck."[16]

Although much about the *Mavi Marmara* incident is disputed, the violent resistence faced by Israel is a historical fact. The article that described the attacks on Israelis as nothing more than an Israeli "account" of what happened, then, amounts to historical revisionism by the newspaper.

Conclusion

New York Times readers were deprived of the information necessary for a clear understanding of events surrounding the *Mavi Marmara* incident and the Palmer Report.

Because most stories that mentioned Israel's use of arms ignored the activist violence that precipitated the confrontation, the false impression left by the coverage is that Israeli naval commandos boarded the ship and opened fire on peaceful noncombatants. And because of the newspaper's selective reporting on the conclusions of the Palmer Report, readers were left unaware of the fact that the Palmer Report directed substantial criticism toward the activists and organizers of the flotilla.

Journalists sometimes point to space constraints to defend the omission of certain facts and views. But if the Israeli resort to force on the *Mavi Marmara* was an important topic during the study period, then the passengers' assault on Israeli troops was an integral part of that story.

At any rate, the newspaper could have fully informed readers without increasing the length of stories.

For example, one article noted:

> Earlier this month, [Erdogan] said that Turkish naval vessels would escort aid ships headed to Gaza to avoid a repetition of a confrontation last year, when eight Turks and one Turkish-American were killed by Israeli commandos.[17] (Sept. 20, 2011)

In the same number of words, this article, which ignored the attack by passengers on the commandos, could have reported fairly about the incident:

> Earlier this month, [Erdogan] said Turkish naval vessels would escort ships headed to Gaza to avoid a repetition of a 2010 confrontation, when Turkish activists attacked Israeli commandos, whose response killed eight Turks and one Turkish-American.

---

1. Amos Harel, "Israel Navy: 3 commandos nearly taken hostage in Gaza flotilla raid," *Ha'aretz*, June 4, 2010, http://www.haaretz.com/print-edition/news/israel-navy-3-commandos-nearly-taken-hostage-in-gaza-flotilla-raid-1.294114; Yaakov Katz, "'We had no choice,'" *The Jerusalem Post*, June 4, 2010, http://www.jpost.com/Israel/Article.aspx?id=177445.
2. Owen Matthews, "The Erdogan Doctrine; Turkey's prime minister is out to rescue," *Newsweek* international edition, Sept. 19, 2011.
3. United Nations, *Report of the Secretary-General's Panel of Inquiry on the 31 May 2010 Flotilla Incident*.
4. Sebnem Arsu, "Turkish Paper Lists Israelis It Says Were in Flotilla Raid," Sept. 27, 2011.
5. Heba Afify and David Kirkpatrick,"Raid on Egyptian Al Jazeera Affiliate Seen as Part of a Broader Crackdown," Sept. 12, 2011.
6. Ethan Bronner, "Setting Sail On Gaza's Sea of Spin," July 3, 2011.
7. *Report*, 4-5. The Palmer Report has 9 points of summary under the heading "Facts, Circumstances and Context of the Incident."

8. "Diplomatic Strains Intensify Between Turkey and Israel," Sept. 6, 2011.
9. Neil MacFarquhar and Ethan Bronner, "U.N. Faults Israel On Flotilla Raid, Not On Blockade," Sept. 2, 2011.
10. Sebnem Arsu and Alan Cowell, "Turkey Expels Israeli Envoy In Dispute Over Raid," Sept. 3, 2011.
11. "Israel Says It Won't Apologize to Turkey for Deadly Flotilla Raid," Aug. 18, 2011.
12. "'Peace activists' stabbing IDF soldier," YouTube video, from Channel 2 (Israel), posted by "ElderofZiyon2," May 31, 2010, http://youtu.be/buzOWKxN2co; "Close-Up Footage of *Mavi Marmara* Passengers Attacking IDF Soldiers (With Sound)" and "Demonstrators Use Violence Against Israeli Navy Soldiers Attempting to Board Ship," YouTube videos, posted by "idfnadesk," May 31, 2010, http://youtu.be/0LulDJh4fWI, http://youtu.be/bU12KW-XyZE.
13. "British Naval analyst on Flotilla lynch of Israelis," YouTube video, from Channel 4 (UK), posted by StandWithUs, June 1, 2010, http://youtu.be/qG0EfG8mnAo.
14. Sefik Dinç, interview, Sept. 24, 2010, Channel 1 (Israel), quoted in Meir Amit Intelligence and Terrorism Information Center, http://www.terrorism-info.org.il/en/article/18016.
15. Sabrina Tavernise and Ethan Bronner, "Days of Planning Led to Flotilla's Hour of Chaos," June 5, 2010.
16. "Panel Finds Israel's Actions Justified in Fatal Flotilla Raid," Jan. 24, 2011
17. Sebnem Arsu, "Drilling Off Cyprus Will Proceed Despite Warnings From Turkey," Sept. 20, 2011.

Chapter 3

The Gaza "Siege"

The Gaza "Siege"

Summary

As with *The New York Times* discussion of the *Mavi Marmara* incident, the way the newspaper dealt with Israel's control of its border with the Gaza Strip and its naval blockade of the territory reflected a broader tendency to conceal the context of Israeli policies. The result left readers with a false impression of Israel placing arbitrary restrictions on Palestinians.

During the study period, only about one in ten articles mentioning the "siege" or blockade also cited Israel's fundamental purpose and context for those restrictions: preventing weapons from entering, or being deployed from, a territory from which Israel is routinely attacked.

Background Facts

In the summer of 2005, Israel removed its army and civilian population from the Gaza Strip.

Only about one in ten articles mentioning Israel's constraints on Gaza forthrightly explained the reason for those policies.

After PA elections in January 2006 and a round of Palestinian infighting in June 2007, Hamas, a terrorist organization dedicated to Israel's destruction, supplanted Fatah as the ruling party in Gaza. International and Israeli sanctions on the territory followed, including Israeli restrictions on the passage from Israel into Gaza of goods not deemed necessary for humanitarian purposes.[1] Egypt maintained control over its border with Gaza and placed its own restrictions on traffic into and out of the Gaza Strip.[2] Despite this, hundreds of tunnels connecting Egypt and Gaza allowed Palestinians to smuggle weapons, goods and people into the territory, and Palestinians in Gaza continued to fire thousands of increasingly sophisticated rockets and mortars into Israeli towns.[3]

Rockets fired into Israel from Gaza leave trails of smoke.

Lilach Shoshan mourns the death of her husband Yossi, who was killed in an August 2011 rocket strike launched from the Gaza Strip. Israel's naval blockade on the Gaza Strip is intended to prevent such attacks.

In June 2010, Israel relaxed its border controls, announcing a new policy under which products, with the exception of weaponry and dual-use items, could be imported into Gaza. Israeli spokesman Mark Regev explained: "From now on, there is a green light of approval for all goods to enter Gaza except for military items and materials that can strengthen Hamas's military machine."[4]

According to the Associated Press,

> The government said the purpose of the new regulations was to protect Israeli citizens from "terrorism, rocket attacks and any other hostile activity." It said the goal was "to prevent the entry of weapons and war material into Gaza, while at the same time widening the entry of civilian products into Gaza."[5]

In January 2009, in response to the attacks from Gaza, Israel also imposed a naval blockade on the territory. According to the U.N.'s Palmer Report, the naval blockade and the restrictions regulating transfers across the land crossings "are in fact two distinct concepts which require different treatment and analysis," in part because the former "was imposed primarily to enable a legally sound basis for Israel to exert control over ships attempting to reach Gaza with weapons and related goods."[6]

Indeed, on more than one occasion, ships, including the Santorini in 2001, the Karine A in 2002 and the Abu Hassan in 2003, attempted to smuggle large arms shipments into Gaza.

During the study period, pro-Palestinian activists organized a flotilla whose stated purpose was to break the Israeli blockade and sail to Gaza. They failed to reach Gaza, but succeeded in garnering extensive media coverage.

Despite its implementation of the naval blockade, which the Palmer Report explained was legitimate and legal under international law, Israel has noted that ships wishing to deliver supplies to Gaza could dock at Israeli ports and, after inspection, their freight would be transferred to the Palestinian territory. Israel also transfers tens of thousands of tons of material into Gaza every week by way of the land crossings.[7]

In summary, during the study period Israel enforced its naval blockade on the Gaza Strip, while the sanctions governing the land crossings between Israel and the territory, initially implemented after the Hamas takeover, had been substantially relaxed.

Coverage by the Numbers

During the study period, 37 articles mentioned what the newspaper generally described as Israel's "blockade" or "siege" on Gaza. Overwhelmingly, these articles did not inform readers of the reason for the restrictions.

• **30** of the **37** articles mentioning the land and sea restrictions failed to explain that, according to Israel, the restrictions are meant to prevent weapons from entering Gaza.

• Of the **7** articles mentioning weapons, **3** failed to mention that weapons in Gaza, especially rockets, are frequently fired into Israeli towns, and one of these went so far as to cast the accusation as "spin" by Israel which, in the reporter's opinion, "defies a brutal truth."[8] This leaves only **4** of **37** articles mentioning the restrictions that provided a minimum level of essential context necessary to understand the debate over Israel's actions.

The newspaper could have and should have provided proper context when referencing the siege. It managed easily to do so in one passage that pithily noted, "Israel says it maintains the blockade to prevent weapons from entering Gaza, where they can be turned on Israel."[9]

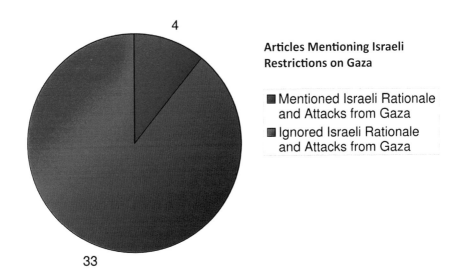

Articles Mentioning Israeli Restrictions on Gaza

■ Mentioned Israeli Rationale and Attacks from Gaza
■ Ignored Israeli Rationale and Attacks from Gaza

But even such a minimal reference was unfortunately an exception. Much more typical was the July 2, 2011 article by Scott Sayare about an attempt by activists to break the naval blockade.[9] The piece quoted an anti-Israel activist stating that she was "shocked [Israel] would be spending so much time, money, energy" to prevent the ships from reaching Gaza, and included many additional criticisms of Israel's policy. But it said nothing about Israel's desire to prevent weapon smuggling into the Strip, the country's stated purpose in imposing and maintaining the blockade. Nor did the article mention that a terrorist organization controls the Gaza Strip or that the territory is frequently used to launch rockets and other attacks targeting Israeli civilians, even though these are essential parts of the story of the blockade that answer the question raised about why Israel spends resources enforcing its policy.

Other articles purporting to give the reason for the restrictions failed to inform readers of the basic facts. For example, a Sept. 12 story by Ethan Bronner asserted that "Israel imposed a siege to try to pressure Hamas, a militant group opposed to Israel's existence."[10]

Far from educating readers, this vague explanation kept readers in the dark about Israel's rationale, while allowing the newspaper to go through the motions of providing context. As noted above, Israel views its naval blockade primarily as a means to prevent weapons entering Gaza, from which those weapons are fired into

Senior Israeli officials inspect weapons found aboard the Karine A. In January 2002, Israel intercepted the ship, which was carrying 50 tons of weapons from Iran to Gaza, before it could deliver its cargo to the Palestinian Authority.

Israel, subjecting residents in the south of Israel to incessant attacks. A central aim of its land border controls is likewise to prevent Hamas from further arming itself. The newspaper should have been familiar with this position, as it was discussed at length in a widely publicized Israeli report released in January 2011, but this story, and many others, nonetheless ignored Israel's concerns.[11]

Editorializing

The newspaper's reluctance to draw readers' attention to the influx of arms into Gaza is exemplified by an article entitled "Smuggling in North Sinai Surges as the Police Vanish," which, as suggested by the title, focused entirely on smuggling from Egypt into Gaza.[12] Stunningly, the piece, which described the smuggling of cars, food, construction material and "a variety of other basic necessities," did not mention a word about weapons smuggling, although just weeks before publication of the article Israel had expressed concern about the illicit import of weapons into Gaza.[13]

While minimizing the threats to Israel, the newspaper overstated Israel's response to those threats. Seven articles during the study period referred to Israel's restrictions as a "siege."

The term is inaccurate. The *Oxford English Dictionary* defines a siege as "the action, on the part of an army, of investing a town, castle, etc., in order to cut off all outside communication and in the end to reduce or take it." This formal definition also reflects common understanding of the term.

But Israel does not, and cannot, "invest," or surround, the Gaza Strip. Although it controls the sea and its own borders with the territory, Gaza also shares a land border with Egypt, and that border is fully controlled by Egypt and Hamas. In addition, Israel clearly does not cut Gaza off from all outside communication, nor does it attempt to. On the contrary, as noted above, Israel facilitates the transfer of tons of goods into the territory every week, it has offered to transfer non-military goods shipped by sea to Gaza by way of Israeli ports, and Egypt allows Gazans to cross back and forth across its border as it sees fit.

In other words, even if anti-Israel activists find it in their interest to use inaccurate and inflammatory language such as "siege," neither sanctions on certain imports and exports across one's own border nor Israel's naval blockade can properly be defined as siege, and a newspaper striving for precision, accuracy and objectivity should avoid such language.

Conclusion

Once again, *The New York Times* failed to properly inform readers on a topic of central importance during the study period. And once again this failure cannot be blamed on space considerations.

Only a tiny minority of articles mentioning Israel's constraints on Gaza forthrightly explained the reason for those policies. As a result, readers often see Israel acting gratuitously and harshly against Gaza, "pressuring" Hamas and imposing a "siege," but are rarely exposed to the ongoing Palestinian violence that prompted that reaction—the relentless rocket fire into Israeli towns, the smuggling of advanced weaponry, and the cross-border terrorist infiltrations from Gaza.

New York Times readers often see Israel acting harshly against Gaza, "pressuring" Hamas and imposing a "siege," but are rarely exposed to the ongoing Palestinian violence that prompted that reaction.

The newspaper could easily have provided proper context in its discussions about Israeli restrictions without affecting the length of articles. Certainly, articles that failed to explain that the sanctions were imposed to prevent the import of weapons included much less important details. There was enough room in one story cited above, for example, to inform readers that a passenger on a flotilla ship was a "ponytailed Norwegian photographer."

And just as another article made sure to mention that Gaza's economy saw dramatic growth only "because it had been at an anemic level during the Israeli siege of the past few years," there surely was room for Israel's basic position about the "siege" to be accurately explained. The newspaper, however, only made space for the former.

1. Israel Ministry of Foreign Affairs, "Security Cabinet declares Gaza hostile territory," Sept. 19, 2007, http://www.mfa.gov.il/MFA/Government/Communiques/2007/Security+Cabinet+declares+Gaza+hostile+territory+19-Sep-2007.htm.
2. Gilead Ini, "Backgrounder: The Rafah Crossing and Restrictions on Cross-Border Movement for Gaza Palestinians," Committee for Accuracy in Middle East Reporting in America, Oct. 22, 2008, http://www.camera.org/index.asp?x_context=6&x_article=1549.
3. Karen Laub, "Tunnel smuggling is booming in Gaza," Associated Press, Oct. 7, 2008; "Rocket Attacks on Israel From Gaza," the official blog of the Israel Defense Forces, last modified Aug. 12, 2012, http://www.idfblog.com/facts-figures/rocket-attacks-toward-israel.
4. Mark Lavie, "Israel drafting new list of goods banned from Gaza," Associated Press, June 20, 2010.
5. Ibid.
6. United Nations, Report of the Secretary-General's Panel of Inquiry on the 31 May 2010 Flotilla Incident, 39.
7. See, e.g., "Gaza Economy," IDF Blog, last modified July 26, 2012, http://www.idfblog.com/category/facts-figures/aid-to-gaza; and "Infographic: Last Week 20,562 Tons of Good and Gas Entered Gaza," IDF Blog, March 20, 2012, www.idfblog.com/2012/03/20/week-alone-20562-tons-good-gas-entered-gaza.
8. Isabel Kershner, "Israel Intercepts 2 Boats Challenging Blockade of Gaza; No Violence Is Reported," Nov. 5, 2011.
9. "As Flotilla's Problems Mount, Activists See Hand of Israel," July 2, 2011.
10. "Reports See Fiscal Woes Undermining Palestinians," Sept. 12, 2011.
11. State of Israel, report of The Public Commission to Examine the Maritime Incident of 31 May 2010 (The Turkel Commission), 53, 71, http://www.turkel-committee.gov.il/files/wordocs/8808report-eng.pdf. "As evidenced by the testimonies that the Commission heard, the land crossings policy sought to achieve two goals: a security goal of preventing the entry of weapons, ammunition and military supplies into the Gaza Strip in order to reduce the Hamas' attacks on Israel and its citizens, and a broader strategic goal of 'indirect economic warfare,' whose purpose is to restrict the Hamas' economic ability ... to take military action against Israel."
12. David D. Kirkpatrick, "Smuggling in North Sinai Surges as the Police Vanish," Aug. 15, 2011.
13. Dan Williams, "Israel sees Libya as new source of arms for Gaza," Reuters, July 21, 2011.

Chapter 4

Violence Double Standards

sidents examine damage from a rocket that landed in a
rking lot near an apartment complex in Ashdod, Israel
Oct. 29, 2011. This sort of incident receives minimal
verage in *The New York Times.*

Violence Double Standards

Summary

A look at two bloody incidents related to the Arab-Israeli conflict, and the relative emphasis placed on them by *New York Times* editors, is revealing. Although both occurred outside the study period, and therefore do not affect the numbers discussed below, they highlight in a dramatic way the newspaper's double standard regarding violence on both sides.

One incident, in August 2012, involved seven Jewish Israeli teens who were arrested for beating an Arab teenager in Jerusalem. The disturbing and vicious attack left 17-year-old Jamal Julani unconscious and hospitalized for several days. The day after the Israelis were arrested, *The New York Times* published a story about the incident, which the reporter, Isabel Kershner, framed as an incident that exposed the warped morals of youth (meaning Jewish youth) in the Palestinian-Israeli conflict. The article was published on the front page, above the fold.[1] A second, follow-up article, published a week later, also appeared on the front page, above the fold. It broadened the story further from one about a violent incident to a indictment of Israeli society, with reporters Jodi Rudoren and Isabel Kershner telling readers the incident revealed "festering wounds regarding race, violence and extremism."[2]

Jamal Julani recuperating from injuries sustained in a beating attack by Israeli youth.

Another incident, in March 2011, involved two Palestinians, aged 17 and 18, who broke into a home in a Jewish settlement and murdered five members of the Fogel family while they were asleep. Those murdered included Yoav, 11, Elad, 4, and Hadas, a 3-month-old infant. The gruesome attack was shocking even by the standard of Palestinian terrorism during the second intifada. But that attack never made the front-page of *The Times.* An Associated Press brief was published on page 5 the day after the incident, and another more detailed story about the incident appeared the following day on page 16.[3] Neither this story, nor any follow-up stories, cast the incident as one about the morals of Palestinian youth or about Palestinian societal incitement to violence and racism.

The CAMERA study was carried out during a period of relative quiet in the Palestinian-Israeli conflict. Still, coverage was marked by an unmistakable double standard that increased attention on Israeli vandalism and defensive military strikes while downplaying Palestinian violence.

Fogel home following March 2011 massacre by Palestinian youth. Victims are depicted on top.

During the study period, two major terrorist attacks were perpetrated against Israelis, killing six Israeli civilians and two security officials.

There was also steady, ongoing violence against Israeli civilians, including Palestinian rocket attacks on southern Israeli cities and Palestinian stone-throwing assaults on Israelis traveling on West Bank roads. These attacks threatened hundreds of thousands of Israelis and resulted in the deaths of six additional Israeli civilians. A mobile air defense system, an extensive system of alerts and shelters in Israeli cities, fortification of homes and institutions, and the thwarting of attacks by Israel's active defense forces prevented additional loss of life on the Israeli side.

According to a Palestinian monitoring group, 54 Palestinians were killed in Israeli military raids or arrest operations. Of those, the majority were described as "resistance activists," and 16 were labeled "civilians".[4]

Certainly, there were greater numbers of fatalities among Palestinians than among Israelis during the six months of the study, but the majority of Palestinian deaths were militants in the process of perpetrating or planning attacks against Israel, killed in Israeli defensive strikes. By contrast, the Israeli deaths were almost all civilians who were deliberately targeted by Palestinians. This distinction, however, was often obscured—despite the newspaper's references to the killing of "militants"—because the coverage highlighted Israeli strikes.

While *The New York Times* reported on the two largest terror attacks, the ongoing nature and adverse impact of rocket and stoning attacks were apparently not deemed newsworthy. Readers were not given a sense of the constant threat of death under which so many Israeli civilians labor each day, subject to "Red Alert" air raid sirens and a race to shelters at any time of day or night.

And while many headlines referred to Palestinians killed by Israel, not a single headline specified that Israelis were killed by Palestinians. Rocket attacks by Palestinian terrorists were reported as an aspect of Israeli actions, relegated to stories about Israeli military strikes that killed Palestinians, plans for military action against Palestinians, or articles about cross-border exchanges of fire.

Also heavily emphasized in *The New York Times* were the actions of a small group of radical settlers who caused property damage, though no deaths. At the same time, attacks against settlers in general and stonings of Israeli travelers on West Bank roads were de-emphasized, even when they resulted in deaths. Further skewing the coverage was the fact that references to and headlines about violence by settlers were presented as fact in the reporter's voice (even when the identity of the perpetrators was just an assumption) while references to Palestinian attacks against Israel were not conveyed directly as fact, but were attributed to Israeli spokesmen (even when the perpetrators had confessed to their crimes).

The sum effect of this coverage was to direct readers' attention away from Palestinian aggression and Israeli victims onto Israeli aggression, be it defensive air strikes or vandalism and arson by fringe extremists.

While many headlines referred to Palestinians killed by Israel, not a single headline specified that Israelis were killed by Palestinians.

Police examine smashed car on road between Jerusalem and Hebron on Sept. 25, 2011. The Israeli driver lost control of the car and was killed along with his infant son after being hit by a large rock in an attack 2 days earlier. There were no headlines about the incident.

Background Facts

Palestinian Terrorism Targeting Israeli Civilians

Large-Scale Terrorist Attacks

During the study period, two large-scale terrorist attacks were perpetrated by Palestinians. The first, on August 18, 2011, consisted of a series of coordinated attacks near Eilat in southern Israel, carried out by four groups of Islamic terrorists that included Palestinian Gazans and Egyptians. The attacks targeted both Israeli soldiers and civilians. Six civilians, including summer vacationers and a bus driver, as well as a soldier and police officer who had come to assist the victims, were killed and more than 31 were wounded.

In the second attack, on Aug. 29, a West Bank Palestinian stabbed a taxi driver, stole his cab, and rammed into a security roadblock protecting a popular Tel Aviv nightclub filled with teenagers. He then jumped out of the car, shouting "Allah hu akbar," and began stabbing people. Before being tackled and subdued by police, he managed to wound eight more people, three seriously.

Ongoing Violence

Throughout the six-months of the analysis, there were ongoing rocket and mortar attacks by Palestinians from Gaza against Israeli civilians in southern Israel. After a two month lull in rocketing following a ceasefire with Hamas in April 2011, steady Palestinian attacks on Israel resumed, with at least 18 separate attacks in July.[5] Rocket attacks from Gaza escalated after Israel responded to the Aug. 18 Eilat assault with air strikes on Gaza terrorist cells it held responsible. Numerous missile attacks were thwarted by IDF air strikes or intercepted by Israel's Iron Dome, a mobile air defense system, and some of the missiles fell short, landing in the Gaza Strip and injuring or killing Palestinians.[6]

Israeli victims of Palesinian terror during study period, almost all civilians.

During the time period between July-December, 334 missiles were successfully fired into Israel by Palestinian terrorists targeting Israeli civilians in 244 separate attacks.[7] The attacks resulted in the deaths of four Israeli civilians and wounded dozens of others.[8]

There were also stone-throwing attacks by Palestinians on Israeli civilian buses and cars traveling in the West Bank. These assaults escalated in the period surrounding the Palestinians' U.N. bid for statehood, and caused vehicle damage, bodily injury and the deaths of two Israeli civilians, a father and his infant son. Several Palestinians were subsequently arrested for their involvement in this and other stoning attacks. Two of them confessed to throwing stones that struck the driver in the head, causing him to lose control of the car and crash.

Palestinians preparing to launch missiles into Israel. Most Palestinian fatalities were those preparing or otherwise involved in attacks against Israel.

Israeli Military Attacks Targeting Palestinian Terrorists and Rioters

In the Gaza Strip, Israeli air strikes and drone attacks targeted Palestinian terrorists in the process of firing missiles, or believed to be involved in the planning and execution of terrorist attacks against Israelis. Israeli military strikes also targeted Palestinian terrorist training camps, and Palestinians believed to be trying to break through the security barrier into Israel from the Gaza Strip. According to the Palestinian Centre for Human Rights (PCHR), 36 "resistance activists" (terrorists), one Palestinian police officer, and 11 civilians were killed as a result of deadly strikes by the Israeli Defense Forces during the time period of the study.[9] (At least one of those civilians was killed not by Israelis but by a Palestinian Grad rocket that had exploded.[10] There were also discrepancies in some of the descriptions of civilians provided by PCHR compared to those provided by international news agencies.[11]) In addition, PCHR reported 5 Palestinian civilians killed in confrontations with Israeli soldiers in the West Bank. According to local news reports, two were killed during riots and three in IDF arrest operations. Those incidents were subsequently investigated by the IDF.

Palestinians carry body of Islamic Jihad "resistance fighter" killed in an Israeli air strike on Aug. 26, 2011.

Violence by Radical Settlers

Several so-called "price tag" attacks were perpetrated against Palestinians and Israeli army targets, presumably by a small group of "hilltop youth" (Israeli radicals living in houses built without permits on hilltops near established settlements) in response to the dismantling of outposts by Israeli authorities and Palestinian attacks against settlers. "Price tag" attacks included arson and vandalism of three mosques, vandalism of Palestinian cars, the infiltration and vandalism of an Israeli army base and the stoning of an IDF commander's car. The perpetrators were widely condemned across the Israeli spectrum, including harsh criticism by the settler leadership and wider community.

The torching of a mosque in northern Israel at the beginning of October appeared to follow the pattern of earlier "price tag" attacks, but police released several Israeli suspects, for lack of evidence.

Palestinian boys walk past wall scrawled with the graffiti "price tag." "Price Tag" attacks included graffiti, vandalism, and arson.

Investigative journalists questioned how outsiders could have made their way to such an obscure site and then manage to set the fire without being stopped at a location that was totally surrounded by local homes. They raised the possibility that the fire was set by locals, as a result of tribal strife, and made to look like a "price tag" attack. These questions intensified when the home of a local Arab villager was attacked following a TV report in which he expressed certainty that the arson was perpetrated by local Arabs, not Jewish settlers.[12]

Headlines and Editorializing

Israeli strikes or raids that killed Palestinians were usually reported in articles or world briefings that conveyed the information in a headline. But, with an exception cited below that referred vaguely to "casualties," Israeli civilian deaths were not deemed headline-worthy—not even in a world briefing.

- There were 10 headlines explicitly implicating Israel for killing Palestinians:

  Gaza: Israeli Missile Strike Kills Two (July 6, 2011)
  U.N. Report Criticizes Israeli Role in Deaths at Border (July 8, 2011)
  Israel Kills Two Palestinians as Raid in West Bank Refugee Camp Goes Awry (Aug. 2, 2011)
  Israel Kills 2 Palestinians (Aug. 17, 2011)
  Israeli Strikes In Retaliation Kill 9 Gazans (Aug. 26, 2011)
  Gaza: Israelis Kill Militant (Sept. 7, 2011)
  Israeli Drone Strike Kills Militants in Gaza (Oct. 30, 2011)
  Gaza: Israel Kills 2 After Sniper Attack (Nov. 4, 2011)
  Gaza: Israeli Strike Kills 2 Palestinians (Dec. 9, 2011)
  Two Killed in Israeli Attacks as Palestinians Continue Rocket Strikes (Dec. 10, 2011)

- An additional 2 headlines strongly implied Israeli responsibility for Palestinian deaths:

  Israel: Missile Kills Gaza Militant (Dec. 31, 2011)
  Activists Say Tear Gas Canister Killed Palestinian (Dec. 11, 2011)

Headlines Indicating Israeli or Palestinian Responsibility for Deaths

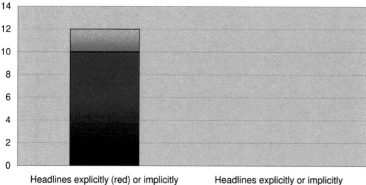

Headlines explicitly (red) or implicitly (orange) implicating Israelis for killing Palestinians

Headlines explicitly or implicitly implicating Palestinians for killing Israelis

• By contrast, no headline explicitly or implicitly referred to Palestinians killing Israelis. The single headline mentioning Israeli victims of a fatal Palestinian attack referred, less precisely, to "casualties"—a term that does not necessarily mean deaths—in the context of a bilateral exchange of fire:

Casualties On Both Sides as Israel and Gaza Trade Fire (Aug. 21, 2011)

• Although dozens of Israelis were wounded in Palestinian attacks during the study period, there was only one headline that referred explicitly to a Palestinian injuring Israelis:

Palestinian Man Injures 8 at Israeli Club, Police Say (Aug. 30, 2011)

• While Palestinian attacks were almost never featured prominently, there was great emphasis on the actions of radical settlers. Several headlines referred either to them or actions attributed to them, but no headlines mentioned Palestinian attacks targeting settlers—not even one that resulted in the deaths of two Israelis.

• There were 11 articles that referred to vandalism and non-deadly arson by radical settlers against Palestinians, including both general references and reminders of previous attacks.

• By contrast, 4 articles included references to Israeli settlers killed in a stoning attack, but only 1 mentioned that the attack was one of multiple such attacks by Palestinians.

Even regarding the major terror attack near Eilat, when Arab terrorists targeted Israeli civilians, the headlines redirected the focus away from Palestinian terrorism against Israeli civilians and onto a general concept of relations with Egypt. The headlines neither referred to the identity of the perpetrators nor to the victims:

Attacks Near Israeli Resort Heighten Tensions with Egypt and Gaza (Aug. 19, 2011)
A Long Peace is Threatened in Israel Attack (Aug. 20, 2011)

• When Palestinians escalated rocket attacks against Israelis in the wake of the terror attack near Eilat, it was Israeli actions that became the focus. One article referred to Israel "**igniting** cross-border exchanges after months of relative quiet."[13] Another article referred to Israeli airstrikes that "**produced** a wave of rocket fire from Gaza into southern Israel."[14]

The terms "igniting" and "producing" implicitly shift blame for Palestinian rocket fire onto Israel. Without information about the steady stream (dozens) of rockets fired at Israel by Palestinians in Gaza in the weeks preceding the Aug. Eilat attack and Israel's retaliatory air strikes, readers are left with the impression that Palestinian rocket fire occurs only as a result of Israeli actions.

• One article recapping the strikes on each side referred only to Palestinians injured or killed in Israeli air strikes. At the time of publication, two Israeli civilians had been killed as a result of Palestinian rocket attacks—one by shrapnel from a Grad rocket and another from injuries sustained in a fall during a Red Alert—and several Israelis were hospitalized with critical injuries sustained in the Palestinian attacks. (One of the injured succumbed to his wounds a few days after the article's publication.) Yet the article mentioned nothing about Israeli deaths or injuries, and instead reported that

> Scores of rockets have hit Israel; dozens of Gazans have been killed and injured.[15]
> (Aug. 27, 2011)

• Unlike the purposeful deadly crimes perpetrated by Palestinians against Israeli civilians, there were no fatal attacks by Israelis deliberately targeting Palestinian civilians. The newspaper, however, never noted this. On the contrary, there was only one mention of "violent crime" in the Palestinian-Israeli conflict and that reference was not to the rockets fired indiscriminately toward Israeli towns, but to the existence of Israelis in territory claimed by both Palestinians and Jews. Bureau Chief Ethan Bronner remarked:

> For much of the world, the very presence of more than 300,000 Israeli settlers in the West Bank amounts to a kind of violent crime. (Sept. 24, 2011)[16]

Double Standards: Facts vs. Allegations

• While Palestinian allegations of Israeli violence were often presented by the reporter as fact, even without corroborating details or evidence, undeniable facts about rocket fire from Gaza were qualified as Israeli allegations.

It is an easily verifiable fact that rocket fire against Israel increased after the Hamas takeover of the Gaza Strip.[17] Yet Bureau Chief Ethan Bronner presented it as mere allegation by Israeli Prime Minister Benjamin Netanyahu:

> Prime Minister Benjamin Netanyahu and his aides have said they are reluctant to withdraw from the West Bank because they say that when Israel withdrew from Gaza in 2005 Hamas took over and stepped up rocket fire against Israel. [emphasis added][18]

In the very same article, however, Bronner presented generalized, unsubstantiated and unverifiable allegations against Israeli settlers as fact:

> In recent months, the militant settlers have burned several mosques and destroyed acres of Palestinian olive and fig trees ...

- The numerous references to violent actions by settlers were almost always presented as fact, but the single reference to the increase in Palestinian stoning attacks was presented as a claim by an Israeli general, not as a solid fact.

- Similarly, the deaths of two Israeli civilians as a consequence of such stoning attacks by Palestinians was presented as an allegation by family members and officials. Never did *The New York Times* relay this as clear fact, and even after the Israeli press reported that the perpetrators had confessed to their crime, the newspaper never shared this information with readers.[19]

- All headlines that explicitly named Israel as responsible for Palestinian deaths relayed this information as fact, even when it was based on claims by Palestinian spokesmen. By contrast, the single headline that explicitly referred to Israelis injured in a Palestinian attack (noted above) qualified it as an Israeli allegation.

Headlines emphasize Palestinian casualties and Israeli actions and deflected focus away from the persistent terror threat that Israeli civilians face from Palestinians.

Conclusion

Palestinian terrorism against Israeli civilians was almost always reported through the lens of Israeli actions. Headlines, word choices and tallies emphasized Palestinian casualties and Israeli actions and deflected focus away from the persistent terror threat that Israeli civilians face from Palestinians. The newspaper could have placed more focus—through headlines or tallies—on Israeli victims of Palestinian aggression but chose to do the opposite. Thus, the distinction between Palestinian violence that deliberately targets Israelis and Israeli defensive actions that target Palestinian terrorists was obscured.

---

1. "Young Israelis Held in Attack On Arab Youths," Aug. 21, 2012.
2. "Israeli Schools Confront Hate After Youths' Attacks," Aug. 28, 2012.
3. "5 in West Bank Family Fatally Stabbed," Associated Press, *The New York Times*, March 12, 2011; Isabel Kershner, "Suspecting Palestinians, Israeli Military Hunts for Killers of 5 West Bank Settlers," *The New York Times*, March 13, 2011.
4. Based on weekly reports of the Palestinian Centre for Human Rights (PCHR), http://www.pchrgaza.org. Some of those described as civilians, however, are described by other sources as having been involved in aggression or suspicious activities when killed. See note 7 below.
5. Based on statistics from the Shin Bet, The Israeli Security Agency, http://www.shabak.gov.il/english/enterrordata, and daily reports of Israeli and Palestinian media.
6. Based on information from the The Meir Amit Intelligence and Terrorism Information Center, http://www.terrorism-info.org.il.
7. Based on monthly statistics from the Shin Bet, The Israel Security Agency, http://www.shabak.gov.il/english/enterrordata.
8. The Israeli Foreign Ministry web site records three deaths. In addition, some Israeli media outlets—Arutz 7, B'Hadrei Haredim, April 24, 2011, and Ma'ariv, Nov. 2, 2011 reported that 62-year-old Varda Nahmias died days after sustaining injuries from a fall she suffered while running to a bomb shelter.
9. A similar example to the above one of the Israeli woman killed as an indirect result of a Palestinian attack is that of a Palestinian civilian reported by the PCHR as having been killed when he fell off his bicycle on Dec. 16, 2011 while attempting to escape Israeli gunfire.
10. A correction published in *The Palestine Monitor* on Aug. 21, 2011: " The original article said that a 12-year-old had been killed by Israeli fire. In fact, as the U.N. OCHA reports

the boy was 13-years-old and was killed by GRAD rocket fired by a Palestinian group."

11. For example, in one comparison, PCHR described "a Palestinian child" with "a mental disability" who was shot by Israeli soldiers on Aug. 16, 2011 while "in an area that had not been explicitly declared as prohibited." International media outlets, by contrast, described the victim as a 22-year-old Palestinian man who had entered a buffer zone and approached Israel's border. And in another example, two Palestinians described as "civilians" by PCHR were reported by Israeli sources to have thrown a mortar shell at the Erez crossing.

12. Eli Ashkenazi, "Shots Fired on Home of Tuba-Zangaria who Blamed Mosque Arson on Locals," *Ha'aretz,* Jan. 16, 2012.

13. Isabel Kershner and Fares Akram, "Casualties on Both Sides as Israel and Gaza Trade Fire," Aug. 21, 2011.

14. Isabel Kershner, "Efforts Seek to Restore Calm Between Israel and Hamas," Aug. 22, 2011.

15. Ethan Bronner, "Israel Faces Painful Challenges as Ties Shift With Arab Neighbors in Upheaval," Aug. 27, 2011.

16. "Amid Statehood Bid, Tensions Simmer in West Bank," Sept. 24, 2011.

17. There are a variety of organizations that record statistics on rocket fire into Israel. They include the Israel Security Agency, The Meir Amit Intelligence and Terrorism Information Center, IDF blog. All record greater numbers and ranges of rockets fired into Israel in the years following Israel's withdrawal from Gaza and Hamas' subsequent takeover of the territory, compared to the years preceding the withdrawal. There are numerous factsheets, newspaper articles and academic studies that cite these statistics and information. A sampling includes: "Factsheet: Qassam Rocket Attacks From Gaza," Factsheet Series No. 35, Canadians for Justice and Peace in the Middle East, April 2008; Barak Ravid, Youval Azoulay, Avi Issacharoff, "Shin Bet chief: Hamas rocket threat from Gaza is mounting," *Ha'aretz,* May 26, 2008; Uzi Rubin, "The Missile Threat from Gaza: From Nuisance to Strategic Threat,"Mideast Security and Policy Studies No. 91, The Begin-Sadat Center For Strategic Studies at Bar Ilan University, Dec. 2011 http://www.biu.ac.il/Besa/MSPS91.pdf; Israeli Ministry of Foreign Affairs, "The Hamas Terror War Against Israel," http://www.mfa.gov.il/MFA/Terrorism-+Obstacle+to+Peace/Hamas+war+against+Israel/Missile+fire+from+Gaza+on+Israeli+ci vilian+targets+Aug+2007.htm.

18. "Israel's West Bank General Warns Against Radicals," *New York Times*, Oct. 12, 2011.

19. Yair Altman, "2 Palestinians Arrested for Palmer Murder," Yediot Aharonot, Oct. 6, 2011; Yaakov Katz, Tovah Lazaroff, "Two Arrested for Throwing Stone That Killed Palmer," Jerusalem Post, Oct. 6, 2011'; Chaim Levinson and Anshel Pfeffer, "Suspects held for throwing stones that killed father, son,"*Ha'aretz,* Oct. 7, 2011.

Ignoring Incitement

Ignoring Incitement

Summary

Palestinian leaders and preachers repeatedly threatened Israel and Jews with annihilation in the most incendiary terms.

According to diplomats involved in mediating the Palestinian-Israeli conflict, a significant obstacle to peace is the refusal of the Palestinian leadership to prepare its people for coexistence with a permanent Jewish state in the Middle East. Yet this newsworthy aspect of the conflict has been largely ignored or covered up by the media.

In his 2004 book *The Missing Peace: The Inside Story of the Fight for Middle East Peace,* U.S. Middle East envoy Dennis Ross provided a post-mortem of the failed peace process, lamenting that PLO chief Yasir Arafat was unwilling to "give up Palestinian myths" or "generate a fundamental transformation" among his people. Instead, the Palestinian leader presented a peaceful face to Israeli and Western audiences, all the while assuring his people that accords with Israel were just a first step in a "phased strategy" to replace the Israeli state with a Palestinian one—an approach that today's Palestinian leaders have actively sought to emulate. As senator, Hillary Clinton denounced what she called Palestinian indoctrination and anti-Israel propaganda, insisting that a "peaceful, stable, safe future" could not be predicated upon "such a hate-filled, violent and radical foundation."[1] And President Obama condemned "Palestinian efforts to delegitimize Israel."[2]

Throughout the six months covered in this study, hate-indoctrination against Israel continued, often in virulent form. Palestinian Authority leaders issued public statements against a two-state peace and celebrated anti-Israel violence. For example, they chose as the face of the Palestinian campaign for statehood at the U.N. a Palestinian woman honored for her role as the mother of several terrorists serving time in Israeli prisons. As figurehead of the U.N. bid, she suggested in an interview with the Israeli daily *Ha'aretz* that the move was just the "first step" toward a Palestinian state that would eventually encompass all of Israel.[3] In the same period, Gazan leaders and preachers repeatedly threatened Israel and Jews with annihilation in the most incendiary terms and ran children's summer indoctrination camps that included paramilitary training.

In addition to paying monthly salaries to prisoners jailed for attacking Israelis, the PA libeled Israel, denied Jewish roots and history in the region, and honored those who murdered Israeli civilians. Such hatemongering—which violates the terms of the Oslo Accords, Camp David negotiations and Road Map peace plan—was a constant staple of programming on Palestinian television, radio and newspapers.

The New York Times, however, deprived its readers of this truth by ignoring or downplaying the extent of anti-Israel incitement by the Palestinian leadership. While the newspaper published multiple articles faulting Israel for obstructing a two-state solution, it only once focused on Palestinian incitement as a possible impediment to peace. And that article minimized the problem, presenting it largely as allegations— some "arguable" and "contentious"—by an Israeli author trying to score propaganda points. While there is no counterpart in Israeli society to the pervasive incitement against Israel and Jews in Palestinian society—there is no Israeli state-sponsored demonizing of Palestinians—*The Times* falsely suggested this was a bilateral issue.

Background Facts

Palestinian incitement against Israel and Jews has been well documented by research organizations including the Washington-based Middle East Media Research Institute (MEMRI)[4] and the Israel-based Palestinian Media Watch (PMW),[5] which record, monitor, translate and analyze Palestinian (and, in the case of MEMRI, Middle Eastern) media, websites, religious sermons and schoolbooks.

Because hate indoctrination is such a profound element in shaping Palestinian attitudes about peaceful coexistence with Israel and the concept of a two-state solution, and because *The New York Times* gave such short shrift to this topic, news consumers missed vital information about a major component of the ongoing Palestinian-Israeli conflict. Enumerated below is a detailed sampling of the government-endorsed incitement that Palestinians were exposed to during the study period.

Indoctrination at summer camps for children

Hamas (Gaza Strip)

Hamas reported record enrollment in 2011 for its summer camps, which are aimed at indoctrinating tens of thousands of school-aged children in the group's militant Islamism and radical political ideology regarding the "liberation of Palestine," jihad, martyrdom and hatred of Israel. Banners at the camps promoted jihad and death for the sake of Allah. Activities included paramilitary training.[6]

Children are given military train
at Hamas summer camp, July 2C

Twelve children killed by Palestinian terrorist Dalal al Mughrabi, who is held up as a hero at Palestinian Authority summer camps.

Palestinian Authority (West Bank)

The PA ran summer camps with divisions named for so-called "martyrs" involved in the murder of Israeli civilians. One camp, under the auspices of Prime Minister Salam Fayyad, catered to children and siblings of terrorists ("Palestine in the Eyes of the Children of Martyrs Summer Camp"), and another was for children of the Fatah youth organization ("Lion Cubs and Flowers"). Its logo included a map of "Palestine" including all of Israel covered by a Palestinian kaffiyeh.

Terrorist Dalal al Mughrabi, notorious for the 1978 Coastal Road Massacre in which 25 adults and 12 children were brutally murdered, figured prominently as a role model at both of these camps. Other terrorists honored at the camp were Abu Iyad, who was involved in multiple terror attacks including the slaughter of 11 Israeli athletes in the Munich Olympics in 1972; Abu Ali Mustafa, who was involved in the planning of terror attacks during the Intifada; and Abu Jihad, responsible for planning multiple terrorist attacks including a 1975 attack on Tel Aviv's Savoy hotel, in which eight civilians were murdered.[7]

Promotion of violence and hatred against Israel

Hamas

Gaza's Al Aqsa TV included malignant proclamations by Hamas and Islamic Jihad leaders calling for the elimination of Israel's Jews. For example, on Sept. 23, Ahmad Bahr, the deputy speaker of Hamas's Parliament, declared that

> Allah imposed the nation of Muhammad, and the Jihad-waging Palestinian people, upon those siblings of apes and pigs [Jews], until we sweep them out of our land and our holy places."[8]

In another broadcast on Al Aqsa TV, on Oct. 25, Khodhr Habib, an Islamic Jihad leader, swore that

> Palestine in its entirety belongs to us. We will not forsake even a grain of its pure soil...We will give you [Israel] nothing but the sword. We will give you nothing but bombs. We will give you nothing but spears and swords, which will slit your throats, Allah willing...
>
> ...and we [will] annihilate this [Zionist] entity, Allah willing."[9]

A televised rally, on Nov. 3, of a pro-Hamas group portrayed the murder of Jews as a religious devotional act:

> You have made our killing of the Jews an act of worship, through which we come closer to you... ...You have made your teachings into constitutions for us – the light with which we dissipate the darkness of the occupation, and the fire with which we harvest the skulls of the Jews...
>
> ....Oh sons of Palestine, oh sons of the Gaza Strip, oh mujahideen– wage Jihad, wreak destruction, blow up and harvest the heads of the Zionists...[10]

A Hamas preacher, on Dec. 2, cited a popular anti-Jewish hadith calling for the killing of Jews:

> Our banner is 'There is no god but Allah,' our slogan is 'Allah Akbar,' our mantle is 'Death to the Jews and to America'...
>
> ...Soon you will hear the stones and trees crying 'Allah Akbar,' saying: 'oh Muslim, oh servant of Allah, there is a Jew behind me, come and kill him.'"[11]

Palestinian Authority

State-run PA TV, often with the endorsement of the PA Ministry of Culture, featured multiple broadcasts of music videos that promoted violence—declaring, for example, that "death for the sake of Palestine is good," requesting guidance on "how to turn heartbeats into bombs" and celebrating the use of weapons and rifles against Israel. A video that promoted the use of gunfire against Israel was broadcast numerous times in November 2011 and included the following call to action:

> The state is only a few meters away
> Oh action-spring, receive and shoot [bullets] continuously
> Change the magazine—there are hundreds [of them]
> Load it into the chamber
> Oh AK-47, make sounds of joy and salute the Elder [Arafat][12]

A televised event applauded by PA leaders and broadcast multiple times during September and October 2011 included the following lyrics from a song: [13]

> Oh Palestinians, the revolution is certain,
> with the rifle we will impose our new life....
>
> ...Oh Palestinians, I want to go and be with you.
> Fire is in my hands, and with you attack the snake's head [Israel][14]

Another event, endorsed by the Ministry of Culture and broadcast repeatedly on state television, featured a song urging violence against Israel:

> He who offers his blood doesn't care if his blood flows upon the ground.
> As the weapon of the revolution is in my hand, so my presence will be forced [upon Israel]. My weapon has emerged, my weapon has emerged.[15]

There were also music videos that encouraged hatred of Israel – for example, multiple rebroadcasts of a song of loathing to a "despicable" Israel that is compared to a "scorpion," sung by an advisor to the PA.[16]

Glorification of terrorists and terrorism

Hamas

Al Aqsa TV interviewed terrorists and praised their actions, especially during the Israeli release of Palestinian prisoners in exchange for the kidnapped Israeli soldier Gilad Shalit. For example, televised greetings to the prisoners by Hamas leader Khalil Al-Khayeh named and celebrated specific prisoners and their attacks against Israelis (including Abd Al Hadi Ghneim's killing of 16 Israeli civilians when he hijacked

Allah willing, you will massacre them like we massacred them in Hebron.

and drove a crowded Egged bus into a ravine and Khalil Abu Elbe's killing of 8 Israelis when he drove into a crowd of civilians and soldiers waiting at a bus stop in Israel).

The Palestinian leader concluded with the following homage:

> In these streets, they would bring the Jews down, one after the other. Let us salute these heroes of the knife, the heroes of martyrdom operations, Jihad, and the resistance.[17]

Palestinian Authority

PA television also broadcast and rebroadcast programs that glorified terrorists and their attacks against Israeli civilians. These included music videos extolling the actions of Dalal al Mughrabi and programs like "In a Fighter's Home," "The Best Mothers," "For You" that featured family members, TV hosts and PA officials extolling Palestinian terrorists as "role models" and "symbols," and lauding their actions as "heroic." Terrorists honored included those involved with some of the deadliest attacks on Israeli civilians—the Sbarro pizzeria attack (which killed 15 and wounded 130 civilians),[18] the Dolphinarium nightclub attack (which killed 21 and wounded 120 civilians),[19] the Passover massacre at a Netanya hotel (which killed 30 and wounded 140 civilians);[20] as well as bus and car bombings and stabbings responsible for the deaths of dozens of civilians and the maiming of hundreds more, including numerous children.

> PA television broadcast and rebroadcast programs that glorified terrorists and their attacks against Israeli civilians.

In July and September 2011, Palestinian Media Watch presented reports to the U.S. Congress and the British and Dutch Parliaments regarding the Palestinian Authority's payment of salaries to thousands of Palestinians involved in terrorist attacks against Israel. PMW reported on a recently passed PA law formalizing the long-time PA practice of paying a monthly salary—exceeding the average salary of Palestinians—to those involved in attacks against Israel. According to the law, salaries would be paid to the families of or directly to anyone (regardless of political affiliation) imprisoned in the occupation's [Israel's] prisons as a result of his participation in the struggle against the occupation."[21]

Claim to the entire state of Israel

Hamas

In a televised broadcast, Hamas Prime Minister Ismail Haniya reaffirmed that the Palestinians would fight to gain control of the entire land of Israel:

> Today, we say, in an explicit and unambiguous fashion: The armed resistance and armed struggle are our strategic choice and our path to liberate the Palestinian land, from the [Mediterranean] Sea to the [Jordan] River, and to drive the usurping invaders out of the blessed land of Palestine...
>
> ...Jerusalem belongs to us, not to the oppressors. Jerusalem is Palestinian, Arab, and Islamic. I don't mean only East Jerusalem. Jerusalem in its entirety is the capital of the state of Palestine, Allah willing...
>
> ...Palestine means Palestine in its entirety, from the River to the Sea. There will be no concession of a single inch of the land of Palestine.[22]

Palestinian Authority

The claim that all of Israel belongs to the Palestinians was repeated again and again in PA TV music videos, documentaries and children's programming, as well as in articles and editorials published in the official Palestinian daily *Al Hayat al Jadida*. Cities and regions inside Israel—Tiberias, Safed, Ashkelon, Haifa, Acre, Jaffa, and Galilee – were described as part of the Palestinian homeland, and Israel was repeatedly referred to in PA media as the Palestinian "interior"[23] or "the occupied 1948 territories."[24] A cartoon published in the official daily on Aug. 21 depicted a map of all of Israel with the caption "the only red line."[25]

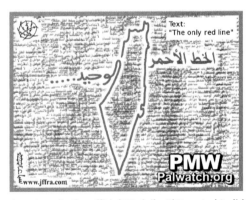

A cartoon in the official PA daily *Al Hayat al Jadida* depicts Palestinian control over all of Israel as a "red line."

Denial of Jewish history in the region

Palestinian Authority

Ambassador Dennis Ross, who presided over President Clinton's Israeli-Palestinian peace efforts at Camp David in 2000, reported that the only idea raised by Yasir

Arafat during the talks was that the Temple had never existed in Jerusalem. Arafat's revisionist history has been reaffirmed by subsequent Palestinian leaders. A recurrent theme in the Palestinian media during the span of the study was the denial of Judaism's historical and religious ties to the region.

PA media referred repeatedly to the "alleged" Jewish Temple and accused Israel of inventing a history in the region. According to a religious column in *Al Hayat al Jadida,* "even the 'Torah' falsified, changed and forged, this is the way of the Jews—they always try to change the real names to other false names in order to erase the [historical] facts."[26]

A Palestinian Authority TV news report on Tisha B'Av, the holiday commemorating the destruction of the Jewish Temples, talked of the "so-called" destruction of the Temple. A PA television documentary on the Western Wall proclaimed that

> [The Israelis] know for certain that our [Palestinian] roots are deeper than their false history. We, from the balcony of our home, look out over [Islamic] holiness and on sin and filth [Jews' praying at the Western Wall] in an area that used to have [Arab] people and homes. We are drawing our new maps...[27]

Both the *Al Hayat al Jadida* and PA TV presented Palestinian archeology lecturer Dr. Jamal Amr denying any evidence of a Jewish Temple near the Al Aqsa mosque and asserting that the Jews "have presented a false history to the world through Josephus, the well-known Jewish historian of the first century CE...."[28] And the PA daily reported on the efforts of Fatah Advisory Council member Ahmed Ghneim to embark on a campaign to Palestinize Jerusalem, noting that "the insistence on declaring Jerusalem the eternal capital [of the Jewish people] means that the war is a religious war, even though Israel has no right to Jerusalem—not religiously, not legally, not politically, and not historically."[29]

Libels Against Israel

Libels promulgated in PA media included the claim that Israel has begun to, or intends to, destroy the Al Aqsa mosque;[30] that the Israeli "occupation" is spreading AIDS among Palestinians;[31] that Israel killed Yasir Arafat by poisoning him;[32] that Israel steals the organs of Palestinians;[33] that Israel carries out Nazi-like experimentation on, and deliberately murders, helpless Palestinian prisoners;[34] that Israel is "flooding Jerusalem with drugs and preventing security forces in the city from acting against the phenomenon."[35]

PA's U.N. Campaign Features Mother of "Shahid"

On Sept. 8, 2011, the Palestinian Authority officially launched its campaign to join the United Nations as a full member state, with a procession to the United Nations office in Ramallah. Leading the procession to deliver an official letter to Secretary General Ban Ki Moon was Latifa Abu Hmeid, chosen as "a symbol of Palestinian suffering." She was thus acclaimed because of her role as the mother "of the Shahid (Martyr) Abd Al-Mun'im Abu Hmeid" as well as of seven sons who were prisoners in Israeli jails. Four of them, one of whom was a founder of the Al Aqsa Martyr's Brigade—designated as a foreign terrorist organization by the U.S., E.U. and others—were serving life sentences for their involvement in the murders and attempted murders of

The Palestinian Authority chose Latifa Abu Hmeid, several of whose sons were implicated in terrorist murders, as the face of the unilateral Palestinian bid for statehood.

Israeli civilians and soldiers. A fifth son, a member of Hamas's Al-Qassam Brigades— also widely designated as a foreign terrorist organization—was killed by IDF special forces after he murdered an Israeli intelligence officer. According to the PA Minister of Prisoners' Affairs, who had honored Abu Hmeid with an earlier award:

> It is she who gave birth to the fighters, and she deserves that we bow to her in salute and in honor.[36]

The celebrated mother and face of the Palestinian U.N. campaign insisted that "We will return to our lands, including the lands of 1948." And when reminded that the U.N. bid was to be recognized within the 1967 lines, Abu Hmeid replied, "But this is the first step. After that, we will want the '48 [borders]."[37]

Statements by Other PA Representatives Against a Two-State Peace

Throughout the study period, high-ranking Palestinian officials expressed opposition to accepting a sovereign Jewish state and to a two-state peace. They made it clear that Arafat's vision of a "phased plan" for Israel's ultimate destruction was not a thing of the past by insisting on what they called a "right of return" allowing millions of Palestinians from all over the world to move into pre-1967 Israel instead of into a future Palestinian state. (The goal of flooding Israel with Palestinians is understood to be a means to eliminate the Jewish state by creating a Palestinian-majority state in Israel.)

In an interview on Arabic TV, PA Foreign Minister Nabil Sha'ath declared that "two states for two peoples" is unacceptable to Palestinians:

> [The French initiative] reshaped the issue of the 'Jewish state' into a formula that is also unacceptable to us—two states for two peoples. They can describe Israel itself as a state for two peoples, but we will be a state for one people. The story of 'two states for two peoples' means that there will be a Jewish people over there and a Palestinian people here. We will never accept this—not as part of the French initiative and not as part of the American initiative.[38]

During the Palestinian campaign for statehood at the U.N., Maen Rashid Areikat, the chief Palestinian representative to the United States, stirred controversy when *USA Today* reported that

> The Palestine Liberation Organization's ambassador to the United States said Tuesday that any future Palestinian state it seeks with help from the United Nations and the United States should be free of Jews.[39]

Realizing that this sort of statement was impolitic for an ambassador to the U.S., Areikat later denied having made such a statement, accused *USA Today* of deliberately lying and pressured that newspaper to reverse the story. However, a recording of the press conference upon which the newspaper's story was based revealed that the *USA Today* report was indeed correct.[40]

Moreover, Areikat had expressed a similar approach in an interview with Tablet magazine the previous year, when he confirmed that "absolutely" all Jews inside the borders of a Palestinian state would have to leave.[41]

While Palestinian officials like Areikat expressed determination not to allow any Jews to reside in the state they were advocating, they just as adamantly insisted that Palestinians currently living outside Israel be relocated into the Jewish state. In an interview with a Lebanese newspaper, Palestinian Ambassador to Lebanon Abdullah Abdullah insisted that a new Palestinian state would not absorb Palestinian refugees from outside that territory because the Palestinians had no intention of allowing U.N. statehood to compromise the eventual return of refugees to Israel. The ambassador explained:

> The state is the 1967 borders, but the refugees are not only from the 1967 borders. The refugees are from all over Palestine. When we have a state accepted as a member of the United Nations, this is not the end of the conflict. This is not a solution to the conflict. This is only a new framework that will change the rules of the game.[42]

Even Palestinian President Mahmoud Abbas proclaimed his opposition toward coexistence with a Jewish state in an interview aired on Egyptian Dream2 TV following the PA's U.N. campaign:

> First of all, let me make something clear about the story of the "Jewish state." They started talking to me about the "Jewish state" only two years ago, discussing it with me at every opportunity, every forum I went to—Jewish or non-Jewish—asking: "What do you think about the 'Jewish state'?" I've said it before, and I'll say it again: I will never recognize the Jewishness of the state, or a "Jewish state."[43]

Coverage by the Numbers

For nearly the entire study period, during which time Palestinians were exposed to a constant torrent of anti-coexistence, anti-Semitic and anti-Israel rhetoric by their leaders, *The New York Times* ignored the phenomenon. By contrast, the newspaper delivered a steady dose of accusations against Israel for obstructing peace. (See Coverage of Peace Talks and UDI)

I will never recognize the Jewishness of the state, or a "Jewish state."

• Only one article during this time suggested that Palestinian inculcation of hatred and rejection of Israel might be an impediment to peace. The charge was attributed to an Israeli representative and presented in the mildest of language:

> A new book by an Israeli watchdog group catalogs dozens of examples of messages broadcast by the Palestinian Authority for its domestic audience that would seem at odds with the pursuit of peace and a two-state solution...[44]

Moreover the article included more criticism of those documenting the incitement than it did specific examples of the bigoted declarations. (See Editorializing)

• There was no coverage of the PA's controversial choice of Latifa Abu Hmeid, the mother of several imprisoned terrorists and opponent of a two-state solution, to represent the Palestinian U.N. bid.

• There was no coverage of the PA's funding of prisoners involved in terrorist attacks against Israel.

• There was no coverage of the Palestinian summer camps run by both the PA and Hamas.

• There was no coverage that quoted any part of the violent anti-Israel and anti-Jewish diatribes by Palestinian leaders.

• And there was no coverage that quoted any of the statements by Palestinian leaders explicitly rejecting a two-state solution.

• Four references were made to the PA's refusal to recognize Israel as a Jewish state, but not one of these references portrayed this as the rejection or obstruction of a two-state solution, as the newspaper repeatedly described Israeli actions.

• An additional article that referred to President Mahmoud Abbas' televised declaration against recognizing a Jewish state referred to it only as an allegation by an Israeli official made to justify the non-transfer of tax payments to the PA.[45]

Editorializing

The New York Times' Article on Palestinian Authority Incitement

The single article on anti-Israel incitement, written by Isabel Kershner, came after

PMW's Itamar Marcus and Nan Jacques Zilberdik published a book about pervasive state-sponsored Palestinian incitement.[46] But the article was less a frank exposé of Palestinian actions than it was about Israelis "finding fault" with Palestinians. Both the headline—"Finding Fault in the Palestinian Messages That Aren't So Public"—and the rest of the article reflected unwillingness by the paper to cover the issue of serious Palestinian malfeasance fully and forthrightly.

The article did not refer to the messages conveyed to children in Palestinian summer camps, nor to the messages conveyed through the PA's funding of terrorists. And it did not cite any of the blunt, anti-coexistence messages broadcast to Palestinians by current PA and Hamas officials and imams.

The story did touch on a few examples of incitement. It mentioned Palestinian song lyrics honoring Dalal Mughrabi, television hosts who cast Israel as being part of Palestine, and Palestinian denial of a Jewish connection to Jerusalem. But these few, brief references did not begin to convey the magnitude and importance of the problem, and no other article during the entire six-month period even referred to Palestinian incitement, let alone to the fact that saturating Palestinian culture with anti-Jewish propaganda is an obstacle to peace and coexistence.

Instead, the article framed the massive evidence against the Palestinian leadership as debatable accusations by the book's Israeli authors while at the same time impugning their motives and attacking the credibility of their charges:

> But for many, the subject of incitement and media monitoring has become as contentious as some of the messages, especially since these pronouncements are often used to score propaganda points...

> This is not a serious attempt to solve the problem of incitement," said Ghassan Khatib, the spokesman for the Palestinian Authority government in the West Bank...

> Some of the examples publicized by the Israeli monitoring group are old ones that have been repeated over the years, and some of its interpretations are arguable...

> ...it is not by chance that those focusing on Palestinian incitement and publicizing it are "rightist groups who use it as ammunition."

At times, the focus was less on Palestinians obstructing peace and more on ad hominem criticism of the Israeli co-author who revealed the problem:

> [Mr. Marcus'] critics, however, note that he is a settler who lives in the Gush Etzion bloc south of Jerusalem, a contested area of the West Bank that Israel intends to keep under any agreement with the Palestinians...

> Some Israelis struggle with the practice of monitoring the Palestinian news media,

A book documenting Palestinian incitement. An article in the *The New York Times* impugned the authors' motives and credibility.

acknowledging the importance of knowing what is being said in Arabic, yet disturbed by how its dissemination is exploited by those not eager to see Israel make concessions.

In effect, the article downplayed the entire phenomenon of Palestinian incitement, by quoting multiple people who justified it as an expected result of a bilateral conflict:

> Some explain the overheated language as a natural expression of such a long-running conflict, and say that any real education in the language of peace is unlikely to come before negotiators resolve the core issues.

> "Reconciliation comes only after matters have been settled," said Radwan Abu Ayyash, a veteran Palestinian journalist and former director of the Palestinian Broadcasting Corporation, the parent of the authority's television and radio stations with headquarters in the West Bank city of Ramallah.

The article further deflected attention from Palestinian wrongdoing by citing critics who falsely suggested there was a counterpart to Palestinian incitement within Israeli society:

> Mr. Khatib said that the authority had significantly reduced the level of incitement on the Palestinian side in recent years. "The question is," he said, "are the Israelis improving or reversing in this regard?"...

> While the Israeli government and news media usually say the same things in Hebrew and English, Palestinians and Israeli critics say they also do little to promote the idea of a Palestinian state. Official Israeli maps do not show the Green Line, the pre-1967 boundary that demarcates East Jerusalem and the West Bank. In Israeli officialdom, the West Bank is routinely referred to by its biblical names, Judea and Samaria. The Israeli education minister recently adopted a plan to take Israeli schoolchildren on trips to a historic Jewish holy site in the West Bank city of Hebron. This summer, the Israeli police briefly detained two rabbis for questioning over their suspected endorsement of a treatise co-written by a third rabbi that seemed to justify the killing of non-Jews, even babies, in wartime.

Of course, referring to "Judea and Samaria" is not merely an invocation of biblical names. It is a correct historical term. In fact, the territory was called "Judea and Samaria" by journalists worldwide until the 1970's, when the term "West Bank" was promoted for political reasons.[47]

Similarly, the implication that it is somehow sinister to teach Jewish schoolchildren about their heritage with field trips to Jewish holy sites, and that this is at all comparable to the genocidal Palestinian rhetoric documented above, is absurd. (It is worth noting that, by contrast, when *The New York Times* covered a clandestine visit by West Bank Palestinians to a beach inside Israel, this was portrayed in an extremely positive light.[48])

And the implication that the arrest of two rabbis suspected of endorsing a book about wartime killings is analogous to explicit calls for violence sponsored, publicized, and even at times engaged in by the Palestinian leadership, is simply wrong. Although it was cast as an Israeli parallel to Palestinian incitement, it would have been more accurately used to demonstrate the opposite: that Israeli authorities question and detain even those suspected of indirectly supporting something that "seemed to justify" wartime killings.

The piece, however, seemed so intent on whitewashing Palestinian incitement and redirecting blame to Israel that it cobbled together a hodgepodge of critics' accusations against Israel to suggest this was a mutual phenomenon.

Whitewashing Hamas

On rare occasion, the newspaper alluded to the fact that Hamas is "sworn to Israel's destruction." But an article by Fares Akram and Ethan Bronner about Hamas's opposition to the PA's bid for U.N. membership cast doubt on the terrorist organization's radical agenda:

> The Hamas charter calls for eliminating Israel, but the Islamist movement's public statements have been vague on whether that remains its ultimate goal. Generally, its leaders speak of full Palestinian sovereignty in the 1967 lines and a 20-year truce without granting Israel recognition.[49] (Sept. 19, 2011)

In fact, the "movement's public statements" have not been vague about whether Israel's elimination is Hamas's ultimate goal. It is not only the group's charter but also its leadership that frequently and vociferously makes clear the ultimate goal is Israel's violent destruction. This is apparent despite the fact that, from time to time, Hamas officials have dangled before the foreign media the possibility that they may be willing to accept a temporary truce with Israel. Such suggestions have been seized upon by reporters who cast it as a sign that Hamas abandoned its radical agenda. But in fact, Hamas's short-term truces have been predicated upon political expediency,[50] do not speak to Hamas's long term anti-Israel strategy, and are typically accompanied by reiteration to Arab audiences that the movement aims to eliminate the Jewish state.[51]

In the passage quoted above, Akram and Bronner apparently alluded to a statement by Hamas leader Ismail Haniyeh made eight months earlier, at a Dec. 1, 2010 meeting with international journalists. There, Haniyeh raised the possibility that Hamas could accept a referendum on a future PLO peace treaty with Israel that would result in a Palestinian state in the West Bank and Gaza.[52] Yet, not two weeks later, Haniyeh released a statement declaring:

> We say that Palestine from the sea to the [Jordan] river is fully the land of the Palestinians. We will cede none of it, and we will not recognize the so-called state of Israel.[53]

Although *The Times* referred to the first Haniyeh statement signaling possible moderation, it never bothered to report on his subsequent statement reaffirming Hamas's underlying vision, nor on any of the other clear-cut declarations by Hamas leaders about their "ultimate goal" of eliminating Israel. Instead, Akram and Bronner continued months later to hang onto Haniyeh's hint of a softening approach to Israel.

Several days after this article was published, Hamas's deputy Parliament speaker spoke of sweeping the Jews "out of our land and our holy places." There was no coverage of it in *The New York Times*. Nor was there coverage of any of the group's genocidal rhetoric during the study period.

Conclusion

By failing adequately to cover what many consider one of the most profound issues in the Palestinian-Israeli conflict—the Palestinian leadership's overt rejection of Israel and the inculcation of genocidal bigotry in the society—*The New York Times* denied its readers information vital for a comprehension of the forces shaping the ongoing conflict. By whitewashing Palestinian incitement generally and failing to cover the most ferocious denigration of Israel and the Jewish people or the inevitable consequences of hate-indoctrination, the newspaper is echoing its historic failure to report the onslaught against the Jews of World War II Europe.

---

1. Press conference, July 8, 2007 (reported by Cybercast News Service).
2. Remarks of President Obama, May 19, 2011 (released by White House Press Secretary).
3. Avi Issacharoff, *Ha'aretz*, Interview with Latifa Abu Hmeid, "In Ramallah they don't want another intifada and are worried about the IDF's reaction," Sept. 16, 2011.
4. www.memri.org.
5. www.palwatch.org.
6. Reported by The Meir Amit Intelligence and Information Center and local newspapers.
7. *Al Ayam*, July 20, 2011, translated by PMW.
8. Al Aqsa TV, Sept. 23, 2011; recorded and translated by MEMRI.
9. Al Aqsa TV, Oct. 25, 2011; recorded and translated by MEMRI.
10. Al Aqsa TV, Nov. 3, 2011; recorded and translated by MEMRI.
11. Al Aqsa TV, Dec. 2, 2011; recorded and translated by MEMRI.
12. PA TV, multiple broadcasts in Nov. 2011; recorded and translated by PMW.
13. According to PMW, the following members of the Fatah Central and PLO Executive Committees applauded the performance: Abbas Zaki, Sultan Abu Al-Einein, Hanan Ashrawi, and Abd Al-Rahim Maluh.
14. PA TV, multiple broadcasts in Sept.- Oct. 2011; recorded and translated by PMW.
15. PA TV, broadcast seven times in Oct. 2011, as well as before and after the study period, recorded and translated by PMW.
16. PA TV, broadcast five times in Nov.-Dec, 2011; recorded and translated by PMW.
17. Al Aqsa TV, Oct. 19, 2011; recorded and translated by MEMRI.
18. PA TV, Aug. 10, Oct. 23, 2011; recorded and translated by PMW.
19. PA TV, Aug. 11, 2011; recorded and translated by PMW.
20. PA TV, Oct. 25, 2011; recorded and translated by PMW.
21. Chapter 1 of *Law of Prisoners, 2004/19*, The Prisoners' Centre for Studies, www.alasra.ps, accessed and translated by PMW, May 9, 2011, included in PMW Special Report, July 26, 2011: "Palestinian Authority glorification of terrorists and paying salaries to terrorists with US money".
22. Al Aqsa TV, Dec. 14; recorded and translated by MEMRI, PMW.
23. For example, in *Al-Hayat Al-Jadida* July 5, 2011, Nov. 20, 24, translated by PMW.
24. For example, in *Al-Hayat Al-Jadida* , July 20, Oct. 4, translated by PMW.
25. *Al-Hayat Al-Jadida,* Aug. 21, 2011, translated by PMW.
26. *Al-Hayat Al-Jadida,* July 1, 2011, translated by PMW.
27. PA TV, Aug. 10, 2011; recorded and translated by PMW.
28. PA TV, *Al Hayat al Jadida*, Dec. 6, 2011; recorded and translated by PMW.
29. *Al Hayat al Jadida*, Dec. 29, 2011; translated by PMW.
30. PA TV, July 26, Nov. 25, 2011; *Al Hayat al Jadida*, Aug. 21, 22, Sept. 28, Nov. 2, Nov. 29, Dec. 4, Dec. 14, Dec. 22, 2011; *Al Ayyam,* Sept. 8, Oct. 31, Nov. 24, 2011; recorded and translated by PMW.
31. Director of Public Health Assad Ramlawi, cited in *Al Hayat al Jadida*, Dec. 9, 2011; recorded and translated by PMW.

By failing adequately to cover what many consider one of the most profound issue in the Palestinian-Israeli conflict— the Palestinian leadership's overt rejection of Israel and the inculcation of genocidal bigotry in the society—*The New York Times* denied its readers information vital for a comprehension of the forces shaping th ongoing conflict.

32. Author Haitham Zu'aiter on PA TV, Aug. 30, 2011; Palestinian National Council Chief Salim Al-Za'anoun Arafat in *Al Hayat al Jadida*, Sept. 25, 2011; Institute Chairman Nasser Al-Qidwa, in *Al Hayat al Jadida*;, Nov. 11, 2011; and on PA TV, Nov. 10, Nov. 11, Nov. 16, 2011; *Al Hayat al Jadida,* Nov. 15, Dec. 28, 2011; recorded and translated by PMW.

33. PA Minister of Prisoners' Affairs in *Al Hayat al Jadida*, July 26, 2011; *Al Hayat al Jadida*, Sept. 11, Oct. 27, 2011; recorded and translated by PMW.

34. PA Minister of Prisoners' Affairs *in Al Hayat al Jadida*, July 6, July 28, Aug. 1, Aug. 8, Sept. 11, Oct. 3, 2011; recorded and translated by PMW.

35. PA TV, Oct. 29, Dec. 31, 2011; *Al Hayat al Jadida*, Nov. 19, 2011; recorded and translated by PMW.

36. *Al-Hayat Al-Jadida*, Aug. 28, 2010; recorded and translated by PMW.

37. Avi Issacharoff, *Ha'aretz*, Sept. 16, 2011. (translated by CAMERA)

38. Arabic News Broadcast TV, July 13, 2011; recorded and translated by MEMRI.

39. Ofen Dorell, "PLO ambassador says Palestinian state should be free of Jews," *USA Today*, Sept. 14, 2011.

40. In answer to a question about whether Jews would be allowed to live in a Palestinian state, Areikat replied: "I personally still believe that as a first step we need to be totally separated. And we can contemplate these issues in the future, but after the experience of the last 44 years of military occupation and all the conflict and friction I think it would be in the best interests of the two peoples to be separated at first." Gilead Ini, "Did Maen Areikat Call for a Jew-Free Palestinian State?," Committee for Accuracy in Middle East Reporting in America, Sept. 23, 2011.

41. David Samuels, *"Q&A: Maen Rashid Areikat," Tablet*, Oct. 29, 2010.

42. Annie Slemrod, "Interview: Refugees will not be citizens of new state,"*Daily Star*, Sept. 15, 2011.

43. Dream2 TV (Egypt), Oct. 23, 2011; recorded and translated by MEMRI .

44. Kershner, "Finding fault in the Palestinian messages that aren't so public," *New York Times,* Dec. 20, 2011.

45. Ethan Bronner, "Israel Halts Payments to Palestinians, Adding to Fiscal Woes," Nov. 24, 2011.

46. Isabel Kershner, "Finding fault in the Palestinian messages that aren't so public," *New York Times,* Dec. 20, 2011.

47. Elder of Ziyon documents the timeline of changing usage with media outlets initially referring to the "so-called West Bank" in the early 1970's and subsequently adopting the term "West Bank" as a proper noun to describe the area by the mid-1970's. As the blogger points out, "there is nothing political about referring to the area as Judea and Samaria. Calling it The West Bank, on the other hand, is purely political—first to make it appear as part of Jordan and later to avoid giving it any Biblical connotation." "Anti-Zionists Freak Over 'Judea and Samaria,'" Dec. 25, 2011, http://elderofziyon.blogspot.com/2011/12/anti-zionists-freak-over-judea-and.html.

48. Ethan Bronner, "Where Politics Are Complex, Simple Joys At the Beach," July 27, 2011.

49. Fares Akram and Ethan Bronner, "A Nervous Hamas Voices Its Issues With a Palestinian Bid for U.N. Membership," Sept. 19, 2011.

50. Hamas leaders have often explained what a temporary truce means to them. For example, former Hamas leader Sheik Ahmed Yassin clarified that "Reconciliation with the Jews is a crime ... If reconciliation means a truce and a cessation of fighting for a specified period of time, Islam allows the imam [leader] of the Muslims to undertake such a reconciliation if he believes that the enemy is strong and the Muslims are weak and need time to prepare and buildup" (Alex Safian, "The Hamas 'Truce' Offer: Genuine or Fake?," Committee for Accuracy in Middle East Reporting in America, Oct. 9, 1997). Similarly, former Hamas leader Abd Aziz al-Rantissi explained in a telephone interview with Reuters that a temporary truce was proposed in January 2004 because it is "difficult to liberate all our land at this stage, so we accept a phased liberation" (Noam Blum and Ricki Hollander, "Forbes Features Radical Professor for Commentary,"

Committee for Accuracy in Middle East Reporting in America, June 24, 2010).

51. For example, shortly before Haniyeh's suggestion of holding a referendum on a PLO peace deal in which a Palestinian state would be set up in the West Bank and Gaza, Hamas leader Mahmoud Zahar proclaimed on Hamas' Al Aqsa TV that Jews "have no place among us...and no future among the nations" and that "the expulsion will come, Allah willing, from Palestine, from the entire territory of Palestine." (Halevi, "Talking to Hamas? - Increasing Expressions of Genocidal Intent by Hamas Leaders Against the Jews," Jerusalem Center for Public Affairs, Vol. 10, #19, Jan. 3, 2011).

52. Adel Zaanoun, "Hamas will accept referendum on peace deal: Haniya," AFP, Dec. 1, 2010.

53. "Hamas reiterates all of Palestine claim," AFP/NOW Lebanon, Dec. 13, 2010.

Chapter 6

No Debate on the Opinion Pages

No Debate on the Opinion Pages

Three quarters of all opinion columns about the Palestinian-Israeli conflict during the study period were negative toward Israel. None were negative toward the Palestinians.

Bias against Israel is blatant on the editorial pages of *The New York Times*. Unconstrained by the need to appear objective and even-handed, the newspaper's editors allow those pages to be used as a forum in which to attack Israel freely.

During the study period, the newspaper's opinion pages came under severe criticism from the Israeli Prime Minister's office for "consistently distort[ing] the positions of our government and ignor[ing] the steps it has taken to advance peace."[1] The Prime Minister's advisor also criticized *The Times* for presenting an overwhelming numerical imbalance of articles "negative" to Israel, with "negative" defined as "an attack against the State of Israel or the policies of its democratically elected government."[2]

CAMERA's analysis focuses on those opinion articles published in the print edition of *The New York Times* that directly address the Palestinian-Israeli conflict over a period of nine months—July 1, 2011–March 31, 2012.[3] It includes three categories of opinion pieces:

1) unsigned editorials by the newspaper's editors
2) commentary by *New York Times* columnists and
3) Op-Ed columns by guest authors

Passages within each article were categorized and tallied. A piece with a majority of negative passages about a particular side was considered "negative" toward that side while one with a majority of positive passages about a particular side was considered "positive" toward that side. Articles that included roughly equal numbers of positive and negative passages about a single side, or roughly equivalent negatives about both sides were considered neutral. (See Appendix I—Methodology)

Three quarters of all opinion pieces about the Palestinian-Israeli conflict during the study period were negative toward Israel. None were negative toward the Palestinians.

In addition, the individual passages within each opinion article were analyzed and compared. While there were roughly equal numbers of positive and negative passages about Palestinians (overall, slightly more positive than negative passages), negative passages about Israel outnumbered positive ones by a factor of more than 4:1. Moreover, more than half of the sympathetic passages about Israel were concentrated in one positive Op-Ed. Those who missed that single article would have been exposed to more than 10 times as much condemnation of Israel as sympathetic portrayals of that nation's circumstances.

There were, in addition, several pieces that did not directly address the Palestinian-Israeli conflict but denounced Israeli society or policies. While

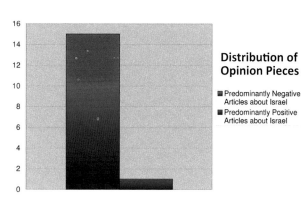

Distribution of Opinion Pieces

■ Predominantly Negative Articles about Israel
■ Predominantly Positive Articles about Israel

they did not fit the parameters of the study and are not reflected in the numbers, they amplified the editorial pages' relentless condemnation of Israel.

Perhaps most striking was the hysterical and extreme nature of some of the articles—far from the reasoned criticism one might expect to find in a serious and respectable newspaper.

By the Numbers

Overall

- 75% of opinion pieces (**15** of **20**) were negative toward Israel.

- **One** piece was positive toward Israel.

- There were no articles negative toward the Palestinians.

- **One** article was positive toward the Palestinians.

- There were **124** negative passages about Israel or its prime minister compared to **29** positive ones.

- By contrast, there were only **17** negative passages about Palestinians or its leaders, compared to **22** positive ones.

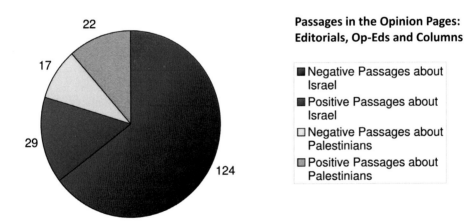

Passages in the Opinion Pages: Editorials, Op-Eds and Columns

- ■ Negative Passages about Israel
- ■ Positive Passages about Israel
- □ Negative Passages about Palestinians
- ▨ Positive Passages about Palestinians

These results can be further broken down by category.

Unsigned Editorials

According to Gail Collins, former editorial page editor for *The New York Times*,

> The editorials are composed by a board of 16 with very specific beliefs and political views, reflecting values that in some cases the paper's editorial writers have been championing for a century. The goal is to convince you, not give you the opposition's best argument.[4]

The goal of *The New York Times* editorial board is evidently to convince readers that Israel is to blame for the Palestinian-Israeli conflict.

- Of 7 unsigned editorials discussing the Palestinian-Israeli conflict, **6** were "negative" toward Israel and **1** was neutral.

- There were no editorials negative or positive toward the Palestinians.

- Within these editorials, **30** passages conveyed criticism about Israel, compared to only **2** that were positive.

- By contrast, only **4** passages conveyed criticism about the Palestinians, compared to **5** that were positive.

With single-mindedness, the newspaper's editorial writers excluded mention of even the most obvious factual counterpoint to their harsh denunciations of the Israeli leadership. Thus they did not mention Israeli Prime Minister Netanyahu's repeated entreaties to Palestinian President Abbas to join together in negotiations without pre-conditions. Nor did they mention the Israeli prime minister's compromise to the Palestinians by imposing a 10-month freeze on construction in settlements. They did not fault the Palestinian leader for abandoning negotiations when the freeze expired. Nor did they blame him for refusing to resume negotiations without pre-conditions. At *The New York Times*, the overarching message was excoriating Israel.

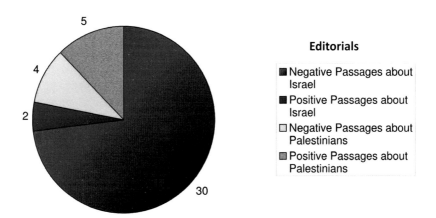

This was the message of an Aug. 8 editorial contrasting the two sides' responsibility for the stalemate in peace negotiations. While the article made a passing nod at impartiality with its statement that "all share blame for the stalemate," the commentary zeroed in on Israel. The Palestinian leader was faulted only for "seem[ing] to give up on diplomacy when Mr. Obama could not deliver a promised settlement freeze" and for not thinking ahead. The passage was, in effect, aimed at the American president, and implicitly at the Israeli leader for not providing Obama with something to deliver.

In sharp contrast to its gentle treatment of the Palestinian leader, the editorial heaped blame on the Israeli prime minister:

Israel's prime minister, Benjamin Netanyahu, has used any excuse he can (regional turmoil, the weakness of his coalition government) to avoid negotiations.[5] (Aug. 8, 2011)

This was a false accusation, but the same charge was repeated on September 12, when an editorial about the Palestinians' unilateral campaign at the U.N. put "the greater onus [for the absence of direct negotiations] on Mr. Netanyahu, who has used any excuse to thwart peace efforts." This time indictment of the Israeli leadership was followed by a directive to the U.S. Congress:

Instead of just threatening the Palestinians, Congress should lean on Mr. Netanyahu to return to talks.[6] (Sept. 12, 2011)

Three days later, an editorial again reiterated that it was Netanyahu who "has been the most intractable, building settlements and blaming his inability to be more forthcoming on his conservative coalition":

...we fear that Benjamin Netanyahu, the Israeli prime minister, will read the [New York congressional] election as yet another reason to ignore the president's advice and refuse to make any compromises with the Palestinians...[7] (Sept. 15, 2011)

And the gist of yet another editorial about the Palestinian leader's unilateral campaign at the U.N. was again blame of Israel, with the same refrain:

The main responsibility right now belongs to Prime Minister Benjamin Netanyahu of Israel who refuses to make any serious compromises for peace.[8] (Sept. 23, 2011)

Abbas's unwillingness to lessen his pre-conditions to negotiate was not deemed a "refusal to compromise."

Even positive developments on the Israeli-Palestinian front became a pretext to blame Israel. An editorial about the release of Israeli soldier Gilad Shalit did not address the cruel and inhumane conditions under which Hamas had held the prisoner for five years—incommunicado, with no access to the International Red Cross. Nor did it discuss the well-founded concern in Israel about the terms of Shalit's release which entailed the exchange hundreds of Palestinian prisoners, many of whom vowed to resume terrorist attacks. Apparently incapable of drawing any fresh, original lessons from rapidly changing events, the editorial board revisited the only message it knew—"blame the Israeli leader":

If Mr. Netanyahu can negotiate with Hamas—which shoots rockets at Israel, refuses to recognize Israel's existence and, on Tuesday, vowed to take even more hostages— why won't he negotiate seriously with the Palestinian Authority, which Israel relies on to help keep the peace in the West Bank?

... Now that Prime Minister Benjamin Netanyahu of Israel has compromised with Hamas, we fear that to prove his toughness he will be even less willing to make the necessary compromises to restart negotiations.[9] (Oct. 29, 2011)

Columnists at *The New York Times* are said to be chosen "for their diversity of opinion." Yet the study found these columnists espoused the same line as the editorialists, reinforcing the newspaper's negative stance toward Israel.

Commentary by *New York Times* Columnists

Columnists at *The New York Times* are said to be chosen "for their diversity of opinion."[10] Yet the study found these columnists espoused exactly the same line as the editorialists, reinforcing the newspaper's negative stance toward Israel.

• Of 6 columns by *Times* columnists discussing the Palestinian-Israeli conflict, **5** were "negative" towards Israel and **1** was "neutral." There were no positive columns about Israel.

• There were no columns negative or positive toward the Palestinians.

• There were **56** passages conveying criticism of Israel and its supporters compared to only **6** that were positive.

• By contrast, **9** passages conveyed criticism of the Palestinians and their supporters compared to **7** that were positive.

There were only two columnists who wrote specifically about the Palestinian-Israeli conflict during the study period—Nicholas Kristof and Thomas Friedman.

According to Kristof, "Nothing is more corrosive than Israel's growth of settlements because they erode hope of a peace agreement in the future."[11] Kristof was silent about Palestinian leaders' public glorification of terrorists who kill

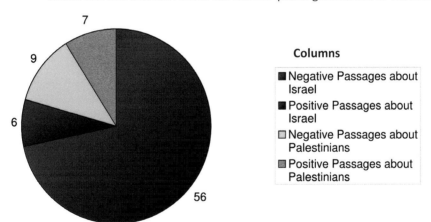

Columns

- Negative Passages about Israel
- Positive Passages about Israel
- Negative Passages about Palestinians
- Positive Passages about Palestinians

Israeli civilians, as he was about the continued targeting of civilians deep inside Israel with rocket attacks from Gaza. He was silent about anti-Jewish rhetoric against the Jewish state by Palestinian political leaders, imams, teachers and journalists alike and he was silent about the adamant Palestinian refusal to accept Israel as a Jewish state.

On the infrequent occasion during the study period that Kristof referred to violence by Palestinians, it was only in the context of "empower[ing] Israeli settlers and hardliners, while eviscerating Israeli doves."[12] That is, murderous attacks against Israelis were seen as negative because they strengthened the talking points of "hardliners"—not because they were threats to Israel. Kristof did not criticize Hamas suicide bombers who have murdered hundreds of Israeli civilians, nor did he condemn the use of Hamas-controlled territory to launch rockets deep into Israel.

In another column, Kristof dismissed the strong support Israel enjoys among the majority of mainstream American Jews and promoted a fringe Jewish organization whose denunciations of Israel echo his own.[13]

Without offering any independent evidence, Kristof championed the self-serving claims of the organization's leader who insisted that only a tiny outspoken minority of American Jews "hijacked Jewish groups to press for policies that represent neither the Jewish mainstream nor the interests of Israel." There was no evidence given to support this claim, and, in fact, it is refuted by polls showing continued strong support for Israel and its policies.[14] However, by pretending that mainstream support for Israel's policies was minimal, Kristof was able to invoke the specter of marginal Zionists controlling American interests—a staple of anti-Semitic bigotry—without appearing to harbor anti-Jewish bias. He asserted:

> Some see this influence of Jewish organizations on foreign policy as unique and sinister, but Congress often surrenders to loudmouths who have particular foreign policy grievances and claim to have large groups behind them.

Thomas Friedman espoused similar unfounded charges with anti-Semitic overtones:

> I sure hope that Israel's prime minister, Benjamin Netanyahu, understands that the standing ovation he got in Congress this year was not for his politics. That ovation was bought and paid for by the Israel lobby.[15]

Friedman's statement that the decisions of elected officials are determined by Jewish bribery, rather than their own views and those of their constituents, was an unsubstantiated and reprehensible accusation of corruption on the part of congressmen and American Jewish leaders. The offensive allegation is belied by well-known facts. With about 70% of Americans positive toward Israel, according to recent Gallup polls, it is apparent that Congressional officials represent their voters when demonstrating support for Israel.[16]

Guest Op-Eds

The newspaper's editors have repeatedly proclaimed their commitment to presenting a diversity of opinion on the Op-Ed pages. Former Op-Ed editor David Shipley insisted that the newspaper tends to "look for articles that cover subjects and make arguments that have not been articulated elsewhere in the editorial space. If the editorial page, for example, has a forceful, long-held view on a certain topic, we are more inclined to publish an Op-Ed that disagrees with that view."[17] The current editorial page editor, Andrew Rosenthal, similarly asserted that editors "are not looking for people who agree with us all the time" and are aiming for "balance over time."[18]

But there was no balance about the Palestinian-Israeli conflict over the study's entire time period—not in editorials, not in columns, and not in guest Op-Eds.

- Of 7 Op-Eds discussing the Palestinian-Israeli conflict, **4** were predominantly negative toward Israel and only **1** was positive.

There was no balance about the Palestinian-Israeli conflict over the study's entire time period—not in editorials, not in columns, and not in guest Op-Eds.

• There were no Op-Eds negative toward the Palestinians, and **1** Op-Ed that was positive toward the Palestinians. (The latter was also negative toward Israel and therefore is counted twice in the chart on page 90).

• Within Op-Eds, **36** passages conveyed criticism of Israel and **21** conveyed sympathy. More than three quarters of the sympathetic passages were found in a single Op-Ed by Judge Richard Goldstone.

This was a change for Goldstone, who is known for heading the notoriously biased U.N. Commission on the Gaza Conflict, for giving his name to a report that slandered Israel and for promoting its unfounded conclusions.[19] Goldstone subsequently repudiated the results of his own commission, and sought to repair the damage he had wrought by submitting an Op-Ed to *The New York Times* recanting the report's conclusion. While *The New York Times* had willingly published the judge's original Op-Ed excoriating Israel, it rejected a submission explaining his change of heart.[20]

More than a year and a half later, however, the newspaper published an Op-Ed by Goldstone refuting "the apartheid slander" directed at Israel.[21] It was the only positive opinion piece about Israel during the entire study period and contributed more than half of the individual positive passages.

• Only **2** passages were critical of the Palestinians, while **10** were positive.

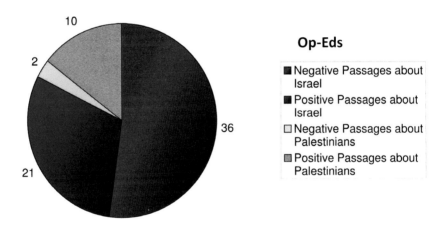

Op-Eds

- ■ Negative Passages about Israel
- ■ Positive Passages about Israel
- □ Negative Passages about Palestinians
- ▨ Positive Passages about Palestinians

Perhaps most striking is the newspaper's departure from journalism in favor of sensationalism. This is most clearly evidenced on the Op-Ed page, by the fallacious claims and extreme rhetoric presented in the name of opinion.

During the study period, this was exemplified by an Op-Ed that offered such a distorted, illogical perspective on the state of gay rights in the Middle East that it appeared little short of a parody. According to CUNY professor and radical activist Sarah Schulman, those who point to Israel's tolerance toward homosexuals are engaged in a "deliberate strategy" to support human rights abuses against Palestinians by making Israel appear "relevant and modern."[22] They are guilty, in Schulman's words, of "pinkwashing."

In reality, Israel is the only state in the Middle East region tolerant of gay men and women. There have been several stories about Palestinian gays fleeing to Israel for their own safety.[23] Islamic governments are especially harsh in their treatment of homosexuals, imprisoning and even executing them.[24] Yet Schulman falsely insisted that the situation for gays in the Arab and Muslim world is not that bad. And the newspaper's editors, in apparent pursuit of yet another anti-Israel Op-Ed, however bizarre, permitted her misrepresentations about a persecuted minority.

The "old gray lady"—a moniker indicating soberness, honesty and reliability – surely has no relationship to the factually shoddy, radical and shrill argumentation that represent the opinions and beliefs of today's New York Times.

Type of Article	Number	Pro-Israel	Anti-Israel	Pro-Palestinian	Anti-Palestinian	Neutral
Guest Op-Eds	7	1	4	1	0	2
Editorials	7	0	6	0	0	1
NYT Columnists	6	0	5	0	0	1
Total	**20**	**1**	**15**	**1**	**0**	**4**

1. "PM Adviser's Letter to 'New York Times,'" The Jerusalem Post, Dec. 16, 2011.
2. Ibid.
3. Because there are fewer opinion columns than news stories during any given period, a longer time frame was used for the analysis of editorials.
4. Gail Collins, "A Letter from the Editor," The New York Times, April 10, 2005.
5. Editorial, "Palestinians and the UN," Aug. 8, 2011.
6. Editorial, "Palestinian Statehood," Sept. 12, 2011.
7. Editorial, "Israel and the New York's Ninth District," Sept. 15, 2011.
8. Editorial, "The Palestinians' Bid," Sept. 23, 2011.
9. Editorial, "Gilad Shalit's Release," Oct. 19, 2011.
10. Gail Collins, "A Letter from the Editor," The New York Times, April 10, 2005.
11. Nicholas Kristof, "Is Israel its Own Worst Enemy?" The New York Times, October 6, 2011.
12. Ibid.
13. Nicholas Kristof, The New York Times, "Seeking Balance in the Middle East" Aug. 4, 2011.
14. For example, a May 2011 poll of more than 1,000 American Jews conducted by Luntz Global on behalf of CAMERA concluded: "The overwhelming majority of American Jews are cognizant of threats to Israel, protective of the country, cautious about risks and strongly opposed to such measures as boycotts, including boycotts of settlements." (PDF of the poll can be found on CAMERA's Web site, http://www.camera.org/images_user/pdf/luntz.camera%20 poll.results.final.pdf) Polls by Dick Morris and Patrick Caddell and John McLaughlin showed similar findings. (Polls cited in: Tamar Sternthal, "Kristof Out to Tea on American Jewry," Committee for Accuracy in Middle East Reporting in America, http://www.camera.org/index. asp?x_print=1&x_context=55&x_article=2094).
15. February 2011 Gallup poll, http://www.gallup.com/poll/146408/americans-maintain-broad-support-israel.aspx; February 2012 Gallup poll, http://www.gallup.com/poll/153092/ americans-continue-tilt-pro-israel.aspx.
16. Thomas Friedman, "Newt, Mitt, Bibi and Vladamir," Dec. 13, 2011.
17. David Shipley, "And Now a Word From Op-Ed," The New York Times, Feb. 1, 2004.
18. Joe Strupp, "Balancing Act," New Jersey Monthly, Dec. 13, 2010.

19. CAMERA, "The Goldstone Report: A Study in Dupllicity," Nov. 3, 2009, Committee for Accuracy in Middle East Reporting in America, http://www.camera.org/index.asp?x_context=8&x_nameinnews=236&x_article=1736;

Ricki Hollander, "A Formal Letter to Richard Goldstone," Dec. 7, 2009, Committee for Accuracy in Middle East Reporting in America, http://www.camera.org/index.asp?x_context=8&x_nameinnews=236&x_article=1764.

20. Ricki Hollander, "The Goldstone Report and *The New York Times*," April 5, 2011, Committee for Accuracy in Middle East Reporting in America, http://www.camera.org/index.asp?x_context=2&x_outlet=35&x_article=2025.

21. Richard Goldstone, "Israel and the Apartheid Slander," Nov. 1, 2011.

22. Sara Schulman, "Israel and 'Pinkwashing'," *The New York Times*, Nov. 23, 2011.

23. "Palestinian gays flee to Israel," BBC News, Oct. 22, 2003, http://news.bbc.co.uk/2/hi/3211772.stm; Dana Weiler-Polak, "Gay Palestinian seeks residency in Israel on humanitarian grounds," *Ha'aretz,* Sept. 29, 2010.

24. "'Death threat' to Palestinian gays," BBC News, March 6, 2003, http://news.bbc.co.uk/2/hi/middle_east/2826963.stm.

"Three men were executed convicted of sodomy," Sept. 6, 2011, Iran Human Rights Official Web site, http://iranhr.net/spip.php?article2227.

Conclusion

The New York Times has an Israel problem. And that means it has an ethical journalism problem—one that has a damaging impact on millions of readers and many other media and policy makers who rely on *The Times.*

If the newspaper wants to restore a reputation for impartiality and fairness, and avoid being viewed as an advocacy organization whose reporting is geared toward championing certain causes, its problematic journalism must be remedied.

Editors and reporters will need to adjust their policies and practices to assure that readers are exposed equally to mainstream Israeli and Palestinian opinions on controversial issues such as the peace process and Palestinian unilateral declaration of independence.

If an editor, for instance, receives a story that repeatedly cites U.N. conclusions that Israeli soldiers mistreated passengers on the Mavi Marmara but never mentions that the U.N. also concluded passengers mistreated Israeli soldiers, the reporter should be told that one-sided coverage is unacceptable.

When reporting on Israel's naval blockade of Gaza or some other military action, editors and reporters will have to remember the Society of Professional Journalists tenet that news stories "not oversimplify or highlight incidents out of context."

They will need to ensure that readers are told about the steady stream of rocket attacks and other violence directed at Israelis, and are fully informed of the genocidal Palestinian incitement that promotes continued violence and murder by glorifying Palestinian terrorists and demonizing Israeli Jews.

If editors do not take steps to live up to the canons of ethical journalism, they should openly admit that impartiality and objectivity is not their aim, and amend their code of ethics currently declaring that "the goal of *The New York Times* is to cover the news as impartially as possible."

And finally, if opinion editors maintain that columnists are chosen for their diversity of opinion and promise that Op-Eds written by outside contributors will make arguments not already articulated, they should adhere to their pledge—or otherwise publicly disavow it.

Readers expect and deserve to hear the whole story. So if presenting the full story, in as dispassionate and balanced a way as possible, is not the newspaper's goal, readers are entitled to know that. Advocacy journalism is, to American sensibilities, unprofessional and objectionable. But promising impartiality while failing systematically to deliver it is the least ethical option of all.

Appendix: Methodology

Scope

The study examines news content directly related to the Paestinian-Israeli conflict in the newspaper's print edition from July 1, 2011–Dec. 31, 2011 and editorial page content in the print edition from July 1, 2011–March 31, 2012. (Because there are substantially fewer opinion columns than news stories, the time scope of the study on editorial content was longer.)

News Pages

Included are the following types of articles about the Palestinian-Israeli conflict and the actions of pro-Palestinian and pro-Israeli activists:

- Breaking news
- News analyses
- World briefings
- Human interest stories

Excluded are articles focusing exclusively on Israel's relations with neighboring Arab countries, Iran, or Turkey outside of their advocacy on behalf of the Palestinians; articles about the U.S. elections; articles exclusively about Israeli or Palestinian internal affairs; magazine articles; arts and culture pieces; and obituaries.

Editorial Pages

The editorial page analysis examines editorial material directly related to the Palestinian-Israeli conflict:

- unsigned editorials
- commentary by *New York Times* columnists
- Op-Ed columns by guest authors

Criteria

News Pages

Every passage in articles meeting the above conditions was evaluated and categorized as based on a variety of criteria.

Criticism

A "passage" can be a sentence, a portion of a sentence, or a series of (usually two) sentences that convey a specific, distinct point of criticism or idea. A passage is considered criticism if it:

- describes criticism being leveled, e.g. "was criticized/condemned for"; "was taken to task for"; "is main problem"
- accuses or implies dishonesty or spin
- accuses a party of violating international laws, borders, civil rights or agreements

- attributes nefarious or provocative motives
- charges or speculates wrongdoing or otherwise disparages
- alleges or insinuates excessive control/power/force over international affairs
- blames one side for a problem

Excluded are statements by the Israeli or Palestinian leadership criticizing their own constituents.

Point of View on Peace Process and Related Issues

A statement by the reporter or attributed to Israelis, Palestinians or non-specified sources such as "supporters," "advocates," or "analysts" that relays any of the following is considered a point of view on the peace process:

- a condition for peace
- a description of a negotiating position or of a position on the peace process (including UDI) or a direct assertion by a partisan attesting to that side's desire for peace or the merit of that side's position
- a reason for adopting or opposing a position
- a rebuttal of the other side's negotiating position or position on the peace process (including UDI)
- blame of the other side for obstructing, undermining or preventing peace

Excluded are:

- statements by identified third parties, e.g. Americans, French, German diplomats, Europeans, Arab League
- statements by Hamas criticizing the Palestinian Authority on peace or UDI
- statements about procedural issues related to peace process, e.g. about which U.N. body to approach first in UDI
- speculation about possible effects of decisions relating to peace process without presenting this as a reason to support or oppose the decision

Editorial Pages

Each passage consisting of an observation, comparison, fact or statement was categorized as either supportive of Palestinians or critical of Palestinians; either supportive of Israel or critical of Israel; or none of those—i.e. neutral or non-applicable.

1. Passages critical or "negative" about Israel met one of the following criteria:

- Singles out Israel or Israeli policy for criticism
- Presents Israel or Israeli leaders or political figures as obstacles to peace or possessing negative characteristics
- Criticizes the American government or citizens for being too supportive of Israel
- Advocates a harsher policy toward Israel alone
- Portrays Israel as unworthy of support or Israeli policies as pushing supporters away.

2. Passages critical or "negative" about Palestinians met one of the following criteria:

- Singles out Palestinians, Hamas or Palestinian Authority policy for criticism
- Presents Palestinian leaders or political figures as obstacles to peace or possessing negative characteristics
- Advocates a harsher policy towards Palestinians alone
- Portrays the Palestinians (PA, Hamas) as unworthy of support or their policies as pushing supporters away.

3. Passages "positive" about Israel met one of the following criteria:

- Expresses agreement or understanding of Israeli policy, behavior or decisions
- Presents a sympathetic portrayal of Israeli society or its leaders
- Presents extreme Israeli groups or behavior in terms that obscure their behavior and ideology

4. Passages "positive" about the Palestinians met one of the following criteria:

- Expresses agreement or understanding of Palestinian policy, behavior or decisions
- Presents a sympathetic portrayal of a Palestinian society or leaders
- Presents extreme Palestinian groups or behavior in terms that obscure their behavior and ideology

5. "Neutral" passages did not meet any of the above criteria, e.g. passages that:

- Addresses conflict without assigning blame or criticizing either side
- Does not advocate change in policy toward either side
- Apportions blame to both sides